CALM IN THE CHAOS

A GUIDE TO OVERCOMING STRESS AND BURNOUT: YOUR BLUEPRINT

BY
NETIERA DANISE

CONTENTS

Most forms of yoga can be amazing for stress relief, but restorative yoga has a few added benefits for this purpose

INTRODUCTION

While stress is a universal experience, persistent high levels of chronic stress can significantly jeopardize one's health and well-being. Chronic stress can worsen anxiety and depression, impact personal relationships, disrupt work productivity, and ultimately lead to burnout and overwhelm.

Stress, Burnout And Overwhelm...

Stress and burnout are often interrelated issues that can have severe psychological and physiological implications. Initially, stress can result in a myriad of undesirable outcomes. Suppose left unaddressed, it may lead to burnout, accompanied by a sense of overwhelm, disrupting both personal and professional aspects of life.

If you find yourself struggling with stress and burnout, this book can assist in identifying symptoms and provide information to help navigate through this challenging period.

Some of the topics covered in this guide include:

- A comprehensive understanding of stress, burnout, and overwhelm.
- The influence of lifestyle choices on stress management.
- Immediate changes that can be made to reduce stress and overwhelm.
- Ongoing strategies such as daily routines, lifestyle modifications, and natural remedies for mitigating chronic stress.

Are You Ready?

Continue reading to discover methods for gaining mastery over your life, minimizing stress, and discovering happiness.

CHAPTER 1
EXPLORING THE IMPACT OF STRESS ON YOUR BODY AND MIND

PEELING BACK THE LAYERS OF STRESS: THE HIDDEN TRIGGERS

Stress manifests in diverse forms, ranging from impacting mental wellbeing and clarity to physical ramifications such as headaches and digestive issues. Although a common occurrence, stress is a serious matter that requires attention and care.

It's essential to approach stress management with the same level of importance as any other health condition. Identifying the root cause of stress is a crucial first step in determining effective treatment. You may be surprised to learn some sources of stress that had not previously crossed your mind.

Not Taking Care of Yourself Enough

Neglecting self-care can result in elevated levels of stress. This emphasizes the significance of prioritizing self-care. This doesn't imply being selfish or withdrawing from social interactions, but rather engaging in activities that benefit you. Taking care of your hygiene, health, mental well-being, and happiness is critical to managing stress levels. It's essential to keep these aspects of self-care in balance to avoid excessive stress.

You Don't Pay Attention to Proper Nutrition

An essential aspect of self-care and stress reduction is maintaining a nutritious diet. This does not imply adhering to a rigid, unsustainable diet plan, but instead, ensuring that your body and mind receive adequate nutrition. Unless you have specific dietary restrictions or allergies, aim for a well-rounded diet that incorporates fruits and vegetables, healthy fats, lean protein, whole grains, and nuts and legumes. Consuming these food groups will provide your body with the necessary vitamins and minerals that help to reduce stress.

Relationship Issues, Even When They Aren't Obvious

It's worth considering the possibility that personal relationships and friendships may be contributing to your stress levels. While some sources of tension in relationships may be apparent, others might be less obvious. For instance, a close friend who habitually exhibits negativity and toxicity while incessantly complaining about their life could be spreading their negativity around.

Though it may not appear to be a source of immediate stress, it might be affecting your emotional well-being and contributing to your stress levels over time. If you find yourself experiencing significant stress, it's essential to evaluate your personal relationships, who you spend the most time with, and how they might be impacting you.

Daily Annoyances That Add Up

Many of us experience consistent everyday annoyances that can accumulate over time. Whether it's being held back at work, dealing with tardiness in your family, or dealing with malfunctions like a faulty water heater, these issues can be frustrating. Although not necessarily life-altering, they can become a significant source of stress. One practical way to manage this stress is by journaling about these issues regularly. By documenting the annoyances, you can evaluate and devise solutions to alleviate the accumulated stress.

Social Media

Social media can serve as a double-edged sword capable of being both a valuable ally and a formidable enemy simultaneously. Despite its advantages, like facilitating the maintenance of long-distance relationships and keeping us connected with friends and colleagues, social media is also capable of taking a toll on our mental health.

Using social media platforms such as Facebook, Twitter and Instagram frequently can lead to increased stress levels without us even realizing it. If you find yourself unable to identify the source of your stress, consider taking a break from social media for a week and observe the changes in how you feel.

Being Messy and Disorganized

Although it may seem insignificant, being a disorganized person can lead to increased levels of stress. Constantly searching for misplaced items, sorting through piles of laundry, or needing to sift through cluttered desks can heighten feelings of stress and overwhelm. Additionally, waking up in an untidy or disheveled bedroom can negatively impact one's stress levels.

Devoting a few minutes each day to cleaning and organizing your living and working spaces can make a significant difference. While perfection isn't necessary, a greater level of organization can enhance your overall well-being.

Signs You Are Not Handling Stress Well

The prevalence of stress among both teenagers and adults has experienced a significant uptick in recent years, with the numbers only continuing to escalate annually. According to the American Psychological Association, the majority of individuals in the U.S. now experience moderate to high stress levels, with over 40 percent of respondents reporting an increase in stress levels over the past few years.

Multiple factors contribute to this rise in stress, ranging from the influence of social media and technology to daily stressors, work, finances, and other significant life events.

Although stress is a common experience, it can become overwhelming, potentially leading to a nervous breakdown or complete burnout. Therefore, it's crucial to recognize when you are not managing stress appropriately. Here are some indicators that you are not coping well with stress and that it's time to take action.

Your Acne is Back

Stress can manifest in various emotional forms, but its physical effects can be inconspicuous. Notably, your skin can serve as a reliable indicator of your daily stress levels. Prolonged periods of stress often cause skin damage, leading to breakouts or exacerbation of pre-existing conditions such as rosacea or dermatitis.

You Constantly Feel Overwhelmed

Do you often feel overwhelmed, as if you can never get a handle on everything? While being busy is normal, experiencing a sense of overwhelm is not the same. When overwhelmed, you feel entirely powerless in managing your life, with an abundance of thoughts leading to feelings of hopelessness and helplessness. This state can lead to an increase in anxiety, depression, and even signs of a mental breakdown, indicating a significant amount of stress that you're not managing correctly.

You Constantly Feel Overwhelmed

Although many of the indications of stress are emotional or mental, they can also manifest in physical forms. Alongside changes in the skin, an individual may also experience chronic pain. Some typical sources of pain related to stress encompass headaches, migraines, backaches, digestive issues, cramping, and various other physical discomforts.

If you're experiencing persistent physical discomfort and there's no identifiable root cause, it's possible that stress may be the underlying factor.

You are Struggling with Low Energy and Lack of Productivity

If you're experiencing a lack of energy, falling behind on work, failing to achieve your goals, and struggling to maintain focus, it may indicate stress is impacting you. Stress can affect your mental state, sapping your energy levels and undermining your ability to sleep. As a result, you may experience decreased productivity, lack of concentration, and challenges keeping up with various aspects of your life.

Your Personal Relationships are Suffering

One of the telltale signs that you are not managing stress effectively is when your personal relationships begin to suffer. Often, this can be a subtle shift that goes unnoticed, as you may be unaware of the changes in your mood or attitude brought on by stress. This could manifest in strained relationships with your significant other, friends, colleagues, or family members. Such changes could stem from various sources, such as a negative attitude or mood, or frequently having to cancel plans due to the stress you're facing.

Your Work Life is Struggling

Finally, it's worth noting that struggling at work can be a significant indicator of poor stress management. In some cases, the source of stress can be attributed to job-related factors, such as an overwhelming number of responsibilities or projects. This can lead to falling behind and difficulty managing personal life outside of work. In other instances, individuals may struggle due to an inability to delegate tasks or take on too much work themselves. It's important to assess one's professional life to determine if stress levels are becoming unmanageable.

Stress Unveiled:
Exploring its Varied Effects on You

When you experience high levels of demands and anxiety, your body responds by producing stress. This can have a negative impact on your physical and mental well-being. Although many individuals may grow accustomed to high-stress levels, it's essential to recognize that such a state is not normal. Fortunately, many sources of stress and overwhelm are unnecessary and can be minimized. It's crucial to understand why reducing stress is necessary before exploring ways to achieve it. Below are some of the ways stress can affect you mentally and physically.

Increases Your Depression

One of the links between stress and mental health is that stress exacerbates feelings of depression. Stress alone cannot cause depression, but it can intensify its symptoms. The reason for this is that stress hormones have a sedative effect, leading to common side effects of depression such as fatigue, lethargy, lack of motivation, poor productivity, increased sleeping, and loss of interest in once-enjoyable activities.

For those clinically diagnosed with depression, stress can be a significant trigger. The surge in stress hormones could trigger depressive episodes, leading to increased stress and more depression or anxiety. The only way to break free from this cycle is to address both the depression and the stress, and identify their origins.

Makes Your Anxiety Worse

Individuals with anxiety disorders such as generalized anxiety disorder, PTSD, or panic disorder are particularly vulnerable to anxiety. Unfortunately, numerous stressors can trigger anxiety and panic episodes, with elevated stress hormones being a common culprit. Furthermore, distinguishing between stress and anxiety can be tricky since they often occur simultaneously and can exacerbate one another, similar to depression.

One effective measure to manage anxiety would be to reduce stress levels. Stress-reducing techniques may help alleviate anxiety symptoms. It's advisable to attempt stress-relief methods initially to evaluate their potential impact on anxiety symptoms.

It Can Cause Personality and Behavioral Changes

High levels of stress not only exacerbate existing mental health disorders but can also lead to various emotional and mental health changes. Individuals may find it challenging to cope with unexpected changes due to the increased levels of stress hormones affecting their mental state. This can cause heightened irritability, agitation, and a decrease in patience. Common behavioral and personality changes resulting from stress include frustration, hostility, bitterness, anger, heightened suspicion, overthinking, and a lack of motivation. These changes can further lead to feelings of isolation, disinterest in activities, and difficulty concentrating on work.

CAN YOU BE ADDICTED TO STRESS?

For those who consistently find themselves stressed and frequently seek out additional tasks, it's possible that they may be addicted to stress. While the idea of addiction to something that can lead to feelings of being overwhelmed and miserable may seem counterintuitive, this may result from a combination of factors such as excessive workload, perfectionism, and the belief that accomplishing more will result in greater benefits.

To learn more about stress, its potential as an addiction, and how to address it, please continue reading.

What Being Addicted to Stress Looks Like

Identifying whether you have an addiction to stress can be challenging, particularly if you've grown accustomed to being in a constant state of stress. For individuals dealing with chronic stress, it can be tough to distinguish between the point at which stress becomes problematic versus something you might be subconsciously seeking out.

Outlined below are some common signs that may indicate an addiction to stress:

01

Never having any free time- Firstly, if you find yourself constantly lacking in free time, it's possible that you may be addicted to stress. Even individuals who lead incredibly busy lives and maintain a jam-packed schedule still manage to carve out at least a small amount of free time. If you have no free time whatsoever, then it's more probable that you are actively seeking out additional responsibilities to fill your schedule.

02

Constantly packing your schedule- It's possible that you are continuously on the hunt for tasks to fill your schedule, even during your free time. Perhaps, you find yourself offering assistance to others, adding extra tasks to your already-existing workload or even attempting to learn new skills on weekends.

While striving to achieve success is admirable, feeling like you must do so is problematic. This inclination could indicate an addiction to stress and the chaos that comes with leading a hectic life.

03

Being bored when you have nothing to do- Do you ever experience a sense of boredom or uncertainty when you find yourself with free time and no specific plans? This could be an indicator of stress addiction, wherein individuals find it challenging to relax and unwind.

04

Feeling more accomplished when you are busier- It's possible that you equate being busy with a sense of accomplishment. However, this mindset is unhealthy. Depriving yourself of sleep, working 80-hour weeks, and neglecting time with loved ones may seem like indicators of success, but, in truth, they lead to burnout and exhaustion. It's essential to recognize that rest is not a weakness but a necessity for both your physical and mental well-being.

How to Get a Handle on Your Stress Addiction- If you find yourself relating to any of the aforementioned symptoms, it might be the right time to address your addiction to stress. The initial step entails acknowledging that chronic stress is an issue you're grappling with, and that you might be inadvertently seeking it out. It's essential to comprehend that stress is common, but not a natural state of being, and that everyone needs a break.

The subsequent measures involve gradually reducing your stress levels in simple ways. This could be as simple as declining one obligation for the week, or setting aside a few hours each week for leisure activities. As you progress, you can gradually work towards an entire day or weekend of rest and relaxation. By implementing these small modifications, you're likely to notice a significant difference in your overall well-being in no time.

05

Being Used to the Feeling of Overwhelm- One of the most severe signs of stress is when it becomes normalized. When stress becomes a constant presence in your life, it can be challenging to recognize its negative effects. You may become desensitized to it and not even realize the impact it's having on you, both mentally and physically.

This may be linked to your addiction, as you continue to add more tasks to your schedule without addressing the stress you are already experiencing.

The Perils of Overthinking: Why It's Best to Take a CHILL Pill

Excessive overthinking, while beneficial in some cases, can lead to a great deal of stress in one's life. This tendency can foster a sense of worry, fear, and anxiety that can be burdensome. It's essential to comprehend the implications of overthinking and how a shift in mindset could help alleviate its negative effects.

Defining Overthinking

Overthinking is a common habit that is easy to fall into and difficult to recognize within oneself. It involves obsessively pondering over everything or specific things in one's life. Overthinking often involves over-analyzing every small detail, constantly worrying about the same thoughts that are often driven by personal fears. Eventually, the constant rumination causes difficulty in making decisions.

While thinking and analyzing situations before making decisions can be beneficial, excessive overthinking can have negative effects on one's life. It can lead to difficulty in finding solutions to simple problems, increased anxiety or depression, and persistent obsessive thoughts that affect one's mood and overall wellbeing.

Why Overthinking is Detrimental to Your Health

Overthinking may be affecting your life in ways you have not realized, such as increased anxiety or difficulty in problem-solving. Here are some reasons why overthinking is harmful:

- Overthinking creates an incessant cycle of negative thoughts that leads to anxiety and depression.
- It causes difficulty in decision-making, leading to prolonged inaction and missed opportunities.
- Overthinking often involves focusing on things outside of one's control, leading to feelings of helplessness and frustration.
- It can lead to physical symptoms such as headaches, fatigue, and insomnia.

In conclusion, while thinking and analysis are essential when making decisions, it is crucial to recognize when overthinking becomes excessive. Overthinking can lead to negative effects on one's mental and physical health, so it's best to find ways to manage it effectively.

IT CAN TRIGGER YOUR MENTAL ILLNESS

Overthinking can have detrimental effects, particularly if you have an existing mental health condition. For instance, if you're struggling with anxiety, overthinking will likely intensify the symptoms. Finding a healthy and pragmatic balance is crucial to managing your mental well-being. The ensuing tips can aid significantly in curbing overthinking tendencies, whether you experience anxiety or depression.

IT MAKES PROBLEM SOLVING MORE DIFFICULT

As previously alluded to, overthinking can impede one's ability to make decisions, causing them to excessively scrutinize every detail and potentially consider unrealistic scenarios. This habit can render seemingly straightforward situations, such as addressing work or personal issues, exceedingly challenging to resolve.

IT AFFECTS YOUR SLEEP

Have you ever experienced difficulty sleeping due to heightened anxiety at night? Overthinking can trigger similar sensations to severe anxiety, leading to perpetual unease. Consequently, it may lead to inadequate rest and sleep deprivation.

Unravel The Mysteries of an Overactive Mind: A Guide to Recognizing The Telltale Signs of Overthinking.

If you're unsure whether you're overthinking, it can be challenging to differentiate between regular thinking and overthinking, which can make life unnecessarily difficult. Here are some common indicators of overthinking:

- **Overanalysis** – Do you tend to scrutinize every conceivable scenario during the decision-making process? This might indicate overthinking.

- **You don't sleep well** - One of the indications of overthinking is poor sleep quality, as overthinking disrupts the mind's ability to rest, leading to insomnia.

- **You get headaches regularly -** Frequent headaches may arise from excessive rumination and overthinking. These symptoms are commonly associated with stress resulting from the tendency to scrutinize every detail.

- **You have a habit of ruminating** - You have developed a habit of ruminating, which involves overthinking and analyzing everything to a significant degree. This tendency can cause a multitude of problems in your daily life.

WHAT YOU CAN DO ABOUT IT

If you believe that overthinking is impacting your quality of life or adding to your daily stress, consider implementing the following actions to mitigate its impact:

Gain perspective - If you find yourself overthinking, strive to gain perspective. Recognize the triggers that lead to overthinking and seek a realistic approach. Are you exceeding the bounds of what is possible in a given situation or suffused with undue stress? Maintaining perspective is crucial when dealing with this habit.

Be more mindful – Mindfulness is a great way to stay present and understand what you have been overthinking, but not allowing them to overwhelm you.

Journal your thoughts - One effective way to manage overthinking is through journaling. By recording your thoughts and reflections, you can unburden your mind and gain a sense of clarity. This process can help you identify the root cause of your overthinking and recognize patterns in your thinking.

CHAPTER 2
DISCOVER EFFORTLESS DAILY HABITS TO ELIMINATE STRESS

DISCOVER THE ULTIMATE DAILY RITUAL TO CRUSH STRESS

Are you experiencing a significant amount of emotional stress that is impacting your physical and mental well-being? If so, it's imperative to take proactive measures to alleviate this stress once and for all.

While stress is a common occurrence, it's not a normal state of being. Medical professionals routinely ask patients about their stress levels since it's closely linked to both physical and emotional health.

One effective way to mitigate stress is by implementing daily rituals that incorporate various habits that promote mental and physical well-being.

Focus on Getting Good Sleep

Adequate sleep is pivotal for maintaining a healthy, rejuvenated, and composed lifestyle. Furthermore, it significantly impacts stress levels. If you're already experiencing high levels of stress, insufficient sleep exacerbates the issue. It's plausible that your inability to fall asleep or maintain quality sleep is a result of stress, which then perpetuates the cycle of sleep deprivation and stress.

By prioritizing quality sleep, you can break this cycle. This might entail disconnecting from your phone at night, establishing a new nighttime routine, or experimenting with natural sleep aids. These changes can help alleviate some of the stress you experience on a day-to-day basis.

"The best bridge between despair and hope is a good night's sleep." - E. Joseph Cossman

Eat Nutritious Foods

As you likely know, maintaining a healthy diet is crucial for weight management, reducing the likelihood of heart disease and stroke, and preventing diabetes. In addition, it can be an effective means of managing daily stress.

While external stressors are often unavoidable, a balanced diet consisting of fruits, vegetables, lean meats, healthy fats, whole grains, and fiber can help to mitigate its impact. Such a diet provides the necessary nutrients to nourish both the body and mind, improving overall stress tolerance.

Go Outside Whenever You Can

Spending time outdoors provides benefits for your mind, body, and spirit. Exposure to fresh air and Vitamin D, both of which are readily available outside, can reduce stress levels. Outdoor activities provide motivation and inspiration, promote relaxation and unwind, and facilitate a closer connection with nature, putting things in perspective and diminishing the significance of stressors.

Incorporating outdoor activities into your routine, such as having lunch outside, taking an extra walk with your pets, or playing in the backyard with your children, can offer numerous opportunities to enjoy nature and reduce stress naturally.

DISCOVER THE ULTIMATE DAILY RITUAL TO CRUSH STRESS CONTINUED...

➔ Trade in Your Coffee for Tea

Regrettably, consuming caffeine can exacerbate stress levels by elevating the production of cortisol, also known as the stress hormone. If you're in the habit of consuming high amounts of caffeine from sources such as coffee or soft drinks, it might be timely to consider reducing your intake. You need not eliminate coffee entirely, but perhaps consider replacing at least one cup of coffee with tea each day. Over time, gradually increase the number of low or no-caffeine beverages you consume in place of caffeinated drinks.

➔ Reduce Technology and Social Media

Have you ever noticed that your stress is worse on days when you spend a lot of time on Instagram or Facebook? This is because social media rarely has good news. Most of the time, it causes stress whether from the latest tragedy in your city or state, political or religion debates, or just drama with people you know in your life or that you work with. Social media can be really toxic, and doesn't help someone who is already dealing with a good deal of stress. Now is the perfect time to start cutting back on using Facebook, Twitter, Instagram, and any other social media sites you frequent.

➔ Have a Nighttime Self-Care Routine

Prioritizing self-care can significantly benefit your mental and physical well-being, particularly if you are experiencing high levels of stress at work or home. Consider allocating a few minutes each evening solely for yourself to unwind and rejuvenate. Engage in calming activities such as listening to soothing music, practicing meditation, cultivating mindfulness, journaling, drawing or painting, taking a relaxing bath, or any other activities that help you unwind and achieve a sense of tranquility.

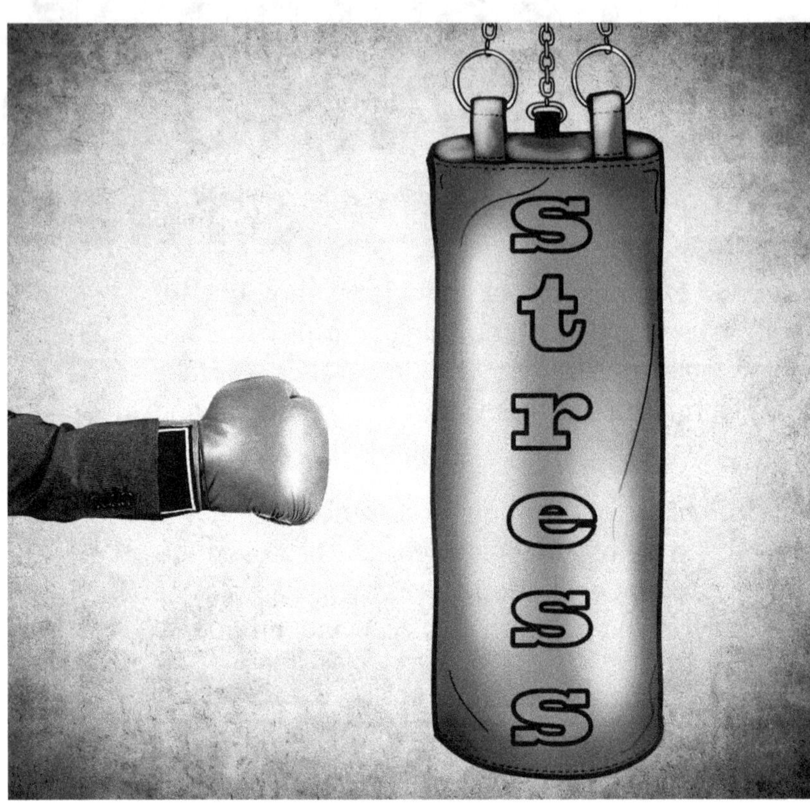

TINY HABITS THAT PACK A PUNCH AGAINST STRESS

If your goal is to diminish stress levels, it's not mandatory to overhaul your entire lifestyle. Often, it's the minor changes you make each day that can lead to noticeable reductions in stress, worry, and anxiety. Moreover, these changes might have added benefits, such as cultivating a positive outlook and increasing overall mindfulness.

Continue reading to discover how you can incorporate small, daily modifications to help manage stress.

Try Guided Imagery

If you're seeking ways to manage stress, you can try the simple and effective meditation technique of guided imagery. This method gradually acclimates you to meditation without undue pressure. Moreover, it provides a powerful means of visualizing your aspirations and fostering positivity, which can be especially beneficial during stressful times.

Guided imagery is often facilitated by an instructor, though you can practice visualization techniques at any time to alleviate stress. The key is to create a scenario that transports you to a serene and calming environment, such as a sandy beach, a mountain trail, or a wildflower garden.

The beauty of guided imagery lies in its simplicity and minimal time investment - just a few minutes of practice each day can go a long way in easing your stress levels.

Adopt Habits That Nourish Your *Body & Mind*

Incorporating healthy habits into your daily routine can be a simple yet effective approach to reducing stress. Certain habits may even exacerbate stress, while others may not have any impact. Therefore, it's vital to prioritize both physical and emotional health when considering healthy habits that work for you and are sustainable. By doing so, you may experience a reduction in stress.

Consider implementing the following healthy daily habits:

Maintain a healthy, well-balanced diet. The food you consume impacts not only your physical but also your mental health. Nourishing your body and mind with a healthy diet can help alleviate stress.

Engage in regular exercise. Exercise is an excellent stress-reliever and a healthy habit that should be a part of your daily routine. It doesn't have to be strenuous or time-consuming. Walking, hiking, yoga, cycling, or dancing are all activities that can count as daily exercise.

Avoid unhealthy habits. Eliminating unhealthy habits is a crucial step in managing stress. Consumption of large quantities of alcohol and recreational drugs may provide temporary relief but exacerbate stress levels in the long run. Furthermore, excessive caffeine consumption can also worsen stress.

Make sleep a priority. Prioritizing sleep is another essential aspect of stress management. Adequate and high-quality sleep is necessary, regardless of your schedule. Sleeping for just a few hours per day is neither normal nor healthy.

Get rest everyday. Taking time to rest and engage in self-care activities daily is also crucial to stress reduction. Scheduling rest and self-care time, even during busy periods, is a priority.

Practice mindfulness. Finally, practicing mindfulness helps to live in the moment and better understand thoughts and worries. Incorporating mindfulness into daily routines, such as during self-care activities, is a healthy habit that can aid in stress management.

STEER CLEAR OF NEEDLESS TURMOIL.

It's possible to encounter sources of stress that are entirely avoidable and optional, despite feeling otherwise. If you're already experiencing an overwhelming amount of stress, it's essential to minimize additional stressors.

To minimize unnecessary stress, consider learning the art of saying "no." You're not obliged to accept every invitation or responsibility that comes your way. Prioritize your time and commitments accordingly. Additionally, assess your current sources of stress and identify any optional factors, such as an extra responsibility you took on, that could be delegated to others.

Dealing with Stress and Overwhelm

Are you currently experiencing heightened levels of stress? If so, it may be leading to feelings of overwhelm. These two feelings often coexist, and if left unchecked, stress can progress to burnout and have adverse effects on one's mental and physical health. Although this is a common experience, it's vital to address these emotions to prevent any further damage. Fortunately, there are several approaches to managing and reducing stress and overwhelm, allowing you to regain control and start living life to the fullest.

Accept What Stress is and That it Can't Be Avoided: One of the primary steps in managing stress involves acknowledging its existence. This is not to say that one must accept stress as an inevitable presence in their life, but instead, to recognize and understand its nature. Identifying the source of stress, defining it, and accepting that it is not a result of one's actions can be helpful in preventing stress from becoming overwhelming. Focusing too much on stress can lead to the release of additional stress hormones, which can exacerbate the issue.

Assigning a name to stress, recognizing that it arises from unavoidable circumstances, and seeking alternative methods of reducing it can be an effective way to approach and manage stress. This shift in mindset can also positively influence how one reacts to future stressful situations.

It's essential to find moments throughout the day to ease both your mind and body when dealing with stress. This can be achieved by practicing simple deep breathing exercises or engaging in more extended sessions of meditation or mindfulness. Such practices will prepare you to tackle stressful situations as they arise, preventing them from escalating and causing overwhelming effects.

When dealing with a specific stressful situation, it's worth considering a different perspective. Take a step back and try to view the problem from a new angle, setting aside personal biases and emotions. This can help in identifying possible positive outcomes, lessons, and multiple viewpoints that may have gone unnoticed. Every experience in life has the potential to teach you something new if approached with an open mind.

RECONNECT WITH NATURE'S ENCHANTMENTS TO REKINDLE THE ESSENCE OF THY SPIRIT.

It's time to regroup and prioritize your well-being. Whenever possible, take a break and enjoy a change of scenery. If work-related stress is getting to you, step outside during your break, go for a walk, or socialize with colleagues during lunch.

Similarly, if you're dealing with stress at home, take a brief respite in your garden or head to a nearby park for rejuvenation. The outdoors offers a refreshing environment with fresh air, sunlight, and new stimuli that can be highly therapeutic.

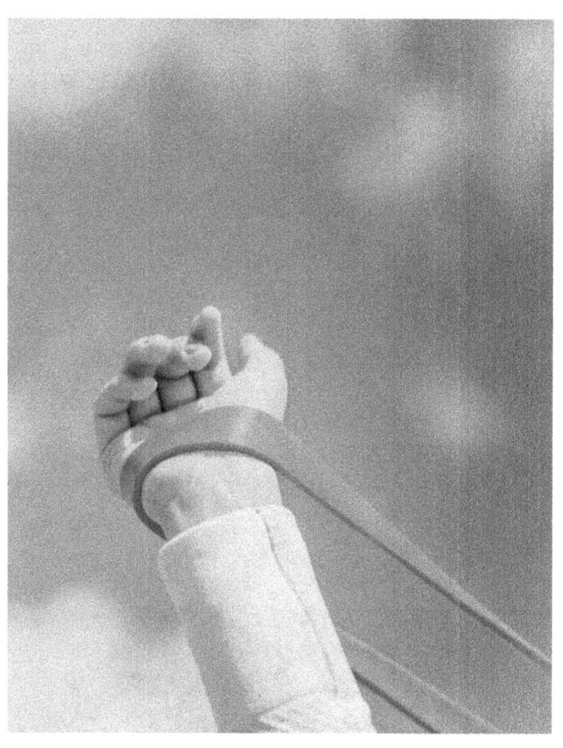

IT'S IMPERATIVE TO ESTABLISH REALISTIC GOALS.

If you're experiencing stress and overwhelm regarding your goals and the process of achieving them, it may be worthwhile to reassess the goals themselves and their feasibility. It's commendable to have ambitious aspirations, but it's essential to ensure they are attainable.

To facilitate this, consider utilizing the SMART method of goal-setting, which emphasizes creating specific, measurable, achievable, realistic, and timely objectives. This approach can help you formulate goals that set you up for success and prevent feelings of stress or anxiety caused by unfulfilled expectations.

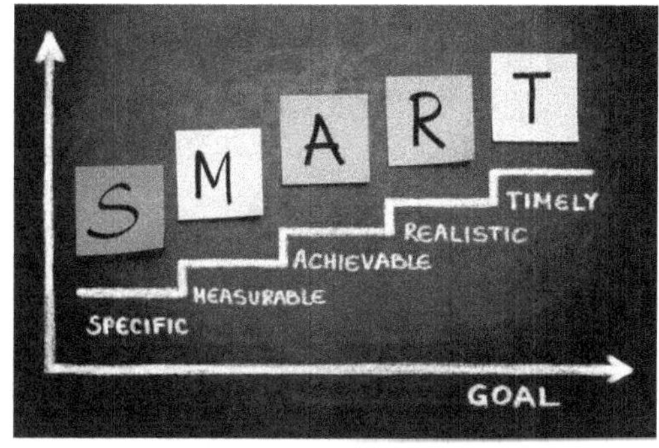

IT'S ESSENTIAL TO RELY ON INDIVIDUALS FOR SUPPORT WHEN CIRCUMSTANCES REQUIRE IT.

It's essential to recognize that no one can achieve everything alone. At times, seeking help, guidance, and support is necessary. It's prudent to reach out to individuals you know and trust who comprehend your situation and can offer solace, rather than add to your burden.

Time Management Tips to Reduce Stress and Overwhelm

Excessive pressure and overwhelming responsibilities can lead to heightened stress levels. Although stressors manifest in various forms, a lack of time management is often the culprit. To alleviate feelings of stress and overwhelm, consider implementing the following time management techniques:

Choose Your Priorities

To optimize your time management, begin by establishing your priorities. Doing so will enable you to tackle various tasks efficiently while reducing stress. Here are some helpful tips for identifying what's most important in your life and what can be deferred until later:

- **Is There a Deadline?**

It is recommended to prioritize tasks that have a strict deadline, as they require completion by a specific date and time. Such activities should be completed first due to their high level of importance. Conversely, tasks without a defined deadline can be allotted a lower priority and tackled later. Attempting to execute all tasks simultaneously can lead to burnout and stress.

- **Look at the big picture.**

It's worth considering the tasks at hand and their intended outcome. Are these tasks essential or merely busy work? Will they add value to your life or help you achieve your goals in some meaningful manner?

- **How do you feel when working on the task?**

If a task is causing increased levels of stress and frustration, it might be beneficial to reassess its priority.

- **Does it affect people in your life?**

It's crucial to consider how tasks may affect your loved ones, whether positively or negatively. Prioritizing responsibilities such as taking your children to their medical appointments or assisting a friend with moving is commendable. However, it's equally important to maintain a balance and avoid overextending yourself.

"If you want to make good use of your time, you've got to know what's most important and then give it all you've got."
- Lee Lacocca.

SCHEDULE YOUR WORK FIRST

To improve time management and minimize stress levels, it's advisable to allocate time slots for priority tasks. This approach helps to avoid the anxiety caused by missed deadlines, appointments, and other tasks that can clutter your mind.

Creating a schedule is a critical step towards effective time management. While it's acceptable to revise the schedule as new tasks arise, it's essential to begin with a clear idea of the tasks that need to be accomplished and when to undertake them. This strategy allows you to make the most of your time.

Does it affect people in your life?

While scheduling your time, it is imperative not to overlook your personal life. Regardless of your occupation or workload, make sure to allocate time for yourself, family, and friends. Failure to do so will likely result in burnout. Therefore, effective time management practices can help you not only schedule your work-related tasks but also ensure you have enough time for leisure activities and personal pursuits.

Start Logging Your Time

Apart from scheduling your time, maintaining a comprehensive log of your activities can aid in effective time management. This practice enables you to retrospectively evaluate how you have been spending your time, discerning areas where you have been productive and where improvements can be made.

For instance, if you feel like you haven't accomplished much in a particular month, your log can help you determine why. You can identify whether you worked excessively long hours, compromising your personal life, or if taking a prolonged vacation impinged on your work responsibilities. Perhaps you are taking extended breaks or inadequately managing your time, which can be rectified with a more structured approach.

Effective time management strategies can differ from person to person, so it might require some experimentation to determine what works best for you, leading to a more balanced life. Avoid merely following someone else's time management techniques, as they may not suit your specific needs.

HOW YOUR DIET IMPACTS YOUR EMOTIONAL STRESS

01

Omega-3 fatty acids are essential for maintaining good health, reducing inflammation, lowering the risk of heart disease, and improving brain function. Salmon, tuna, and walnuts are excellent sources of omega-3s, while olive oil is a healthy source of monounsaturated fats. It's crucial to incorporate these healthy fats into your diet and ensure optimal health.

02

Vitamin D plays a vital role in enhancing energy levels and mood, especially during sunny days. Sunlight is a natural source of vitamin D, and if you reside in a region with frequent cloudy or rainy days, or during winter when sunlight is scarce, you may need to supplement your vitamin D intake through food. Fatty fish, eggs, dairy, and fortified cereal are excellent sources of vitamin D that you can consider incorporating into your diet.

03

To improve digestive health, regulate bowel movements, and manage weight, increase fiber intake by eating more fruit, avocados, and whole grains. Fruits like raspberries, blackberries, and pears provide antioxidants, while avocados contain healthy fats beneficial for heart health. Whole grains such as oats, quinoa, and brown rice are packed with nutrients and linked to a lower risk of heart disease, diabetes, and cancer. Incorporating fiber into your diet is easy by adding fruits and vegetables to meals or swapping refined grains for whole grains.

When seeking ways to alleviate stress, it's natural to focus on workloads, daily responsibilities, and self-care practices. While these are critical, one should not disregard the impact of simple daily choices on stress levels.

Dietary habits, in particular, can either increase or reduce stress. In reality, nutrition plays a more substantial role in stress management than commonly acknowledged, leading to a vicious cycle where stress influences food preferences. Therefore, prioritizing proper nutrition is vital to fuel the body and break this cycle.

NUTRITIONAL DEFICIENCIES

A poor diet can lead to several adverse effects, including nutritional deficiencies that can impact both physical and emotional well-being. For instance, did you know that folate deficiency can cause mood imbalances and even increase the likelihood of depression? Excellent sources of folate include foods like eggs, asparagus, spinach, and avocado. Additionally, incorporating the following nutrients into your diet can help regulate your mood and combat stress naturally:

04

Calcium is essential for healthy bones, teeth, and muscle and nerve function. Almonds, sesame seeds, tofu, and kale are good sources, but sardines, broccoli, spinach, and fortified plant-based milks are also excellent options. Pairing calcium-rich foods with vitamin D can maximize absorption, and it's important for lactose intolerant individuals or those who do not consume dairy to ensure they are getting enough calcium through other sources.

05

Iron is a mineral essential for the formation of hemoglobin, which carries oxygen in the body. It also aids in mental health by regulating mood. Red meat and turkey are good sources of heme iron, while vegetarian sources include nuts, seeds, and leafy greens. Dark chocolate is also a good source. Maintain physical and mental health by ensuring enough iron in your diet.

06

Protein is crucial for building and repairing tissues, maintaining muscles, bones, and skin. It can be found in meat, poultry, fish, eggs, nuts, beans, lentils, tofu, and dairy products. Adults should consume at least 0.8 grams of protein per kilogram of body weight per day, depending on age, gender, and activity level. Eating a variety of protein sources is essential to obtain all the necessary amino acids.

Feeding Emotions with Unhealthy Foods

One more correlation between stress and nutrition is the possibility of using food to alleviate stress and emotional turmoil. The challenge here is the tendency to opt for unhealthy choices. Emotional eating is not a negative coping mechanism if practiced occasionally. Finding a healthy outlet to deal with stress is vital.

However, chronic stress or over-reliance on food as a means of comfort can contribute to overeating, excessive consumption of unhealthy foods, and malnourishment from a lack of essential vitamins and minerals.

STRESS: THE BAD HABIT BREEDER

Experiencing excessive stress in your life can exacerbate unhealthy habits. Apart from vitamin deficiencies and emotional eating, it can lead to overconsumption of unhealthy foods, insufficient exercise, excessive sleep, drinking alcohol, smoking or using drugs. These behaviors can ultimately exacerbate your stress levels, rather than alleviate them.

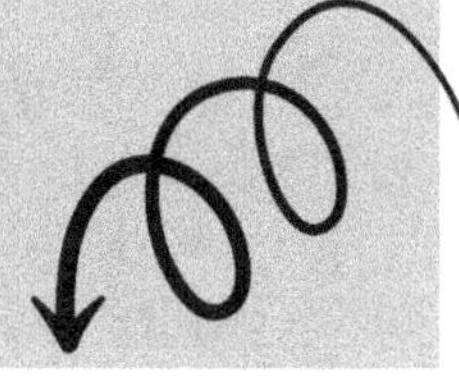

THE CYCLE CONTINUES

The cycle of relying on unhealthy habits to cope with stress is challenging to break free from. While it may provide temporary relief, it can have a detrimental impact on your mental health in the long run. It's imperative to halt this cycle by prioritizing a balanced diet and seeking out healthier alternatives to manage stress effectively. While emotional eating may still be an option, it's essential to supplement it with other healthy habits, such as spending time with friends, engaging in physical activities, or playing with pets.

REDUCING STRESS AT WORK

Experiencing worries and fears is a natural aspect of being an adult, but at times, these concerns may surpass a realistic and normal limit. For some, excessive preoccupation with worries may result in elevated stress and anxiety levels, leading to chronic stress. This condition is characterized by the inability to alleviate stress levels effectively. If you find yourself experiencing worries that are beyond the average level, consider implementing the following tips to help manage these concerns.

IDENTIFYING YOUR WORRISOME THOUGHTS

To minimize daily stress and feelings of overwhelm, it's essential to identify the root cause of your worries. These worry thoughts often lead to burnout, exacerbating the issue. Some worry thoughts are evident, while others are more subtle. The first step is to identify your most significant worry thoughts and seek viable solutions to resolve them. Not all worries may have a feasible resolution, and some may stem from overthinking or inflating the significance of a situation.

ANALYZE AND ALLEVIATE WORRIES BY WRITING THEM DOWN

If you find yourself struggling with stress, worry, or overwhelm, a useful technique is writing down your anxious thoughts. Journaling can help identify the things that trigger your stress and anxiety. Take a few moments to document anything that comes to mind. You might notice that many of your thoughts center around issues that cause worry or concern. This process can be done in one extensive session or by dedicating a few minutes each day to journaling. Over time, you may recognize patterns in your thoughts, such as consistently complaining about the same person, work-related anxieties, or challenges in your home life. Identifying these patterns can help you pinpoint your primary sources of worry.

Know Where Your Main Worries Come From

Now that you have enumerated your worries, it's time to identify their primary source. While it may be impossible to eliminate all sources of stress and anxiety, you may discover opportunities for alleviation.

For instance, if a significant portion of your concerns pertains to inadequate personal time with family, it's worth examining whether your work routine permits flexibility. Is it possible to modify your schedule to accommodate more personal time? Do you work overtime for a specific reason, or is there room for reduction?

Evaluate each of your worries, ascertain the underlying pattern, determine the source, and identify potential resolutions.

Be Mindful to Reduce Daily Worries

To alleviate daily worries, consider incorporating mindfulness practice into your routine. While it may not be a panacea for all issues, mindfulness allows you to recognize your mental state during each activity, fosters a positive outlook, and encourages non-judgmental thinking.

To achieve mindfulness, focus on being present during daily tasks. Pay attention to your surroundings while eating, focus on the task at hand while working, and acknowledge your emotions while driving, walking, or engaging with your children. Being mindful is a useful tool for reducing daily concerns, particularly those founded on assumptions rather than reality.

Practice Breathing Exercises

Incorporating breathing exercises into your daily routine can benefit you in managing anxiety and stress. The versatile nature of these exercises allows you to practice them in any environment. If you cannot perform them at home, there's no harm in taking a few minutes to do so at work. Consistent practice of breathing exercises helps to cultivate a mindful approach to your breathing, which can promote a sense of calm and relaxation, even if it's only for a few minutes each day.

CHAPTER 3 MINDFUL ADJUSTMENTS FOR ACHIEVING STRESS RELIEF

SIGNS YOU NEED A MENTAL BREAK

Do you find yourself grappling with challenges both at home and work, leading to diminished energy levels with little respite even at nighttime? Are you experiencing significant mental or physical changes unrelated to other factors? If so, it's possible that stress is overwhelming your life, indicating the need for a mental break.

However, it can be challenging to recognize the extent to which stress has affected your life, necessitating changes. Here are some common signs that indicate the need for a mental break.

>>> WARNING SIGNS OF AN IMPENDING NERVOUS BREAKDOWN

One of the most prevalent indicators that it's time to prioritize your mental health is when you may be on the verge of a nervous breakdown. These signals are similar to those experienced during periods of overwhelming stress and burnout, though typically much more severe.

A mental breakdown, or nervous breakdown, occurs when stress reaches a maximum threshold. While not everyone experiences a sudden snap, many people reach a point where they can no longer cope. This may result in impulsive actions, such as abruptly resigning from a job or leaving one's current location. Alternatively, it could manifest as an inability to function in daily life.

Symptoms of a nervous breakdown may include severe depression, lethargy, fatigue, excessive sleeping, frequent absenteeism from work, disregard for personal hygiene, and sudden mood swings and angry outbursts.

If you're exhibiting any of these signs, it's essential to take a step back and prioritize your mental wellbeing, identifying the primary sources of stress and taking a break to mitigate their impact.

>>> YOUR ANXIETY OR STRESS HAS WORSENED

Have you observed a recent escalation in your stress or anxiety levels? Perhaps you are experiencing an increase in panic attacks, heightened anxiety, or the absence of moments of respite from stress. These symptoms may signal a need for a mental break. While stress is ubiquitous, no one should endure it 24/7. Your mind and body necessitate a hiatus from stress.

>>> YOUR RELATIONSHIPS ARE SUFFERING

An additional indication that you require a mental break is when your personal relationships begin to deteriorate. This can manifest within a romantic relationship with a significant other or even with close friends and family. When this occurs, it's vital to contemplate the cause of the issue and investigate whether your mood or behavior could be a contributing factor. It's best not to let things linger and instead take proactive measures to alleviate the stress and overwhelm.

Uh-oh, Looks Like Your Work Needs a Boost!

Elevated levels of stress or burnout can impact your work performance adversely, regardless of the type of work you engage in, whether it be attending college, running a business, working from home, or working outside of the home. It's worth reflecting on how you manage your business and how your productivity compares with the past.

Have you experienced any significant changes? Are you completing fewer tasks? Are you experiencing difficulties in maintaining focus and concentration? Are your earnings decreasing? Not only are these indicators of increased stress levels, but they can also exacerbate it, leading to a vicious cycle, which you must address promptly.

You Never Have Time for Yourself!

It's essential to prioritize self-care and take breaks regularly, regardless of your lifestyle or profession. No amount of work justifies neglecting your well-being.

If you find your time is entirely consumed by work, familial obligations, and household duties, without any moments for personal relaxation, it's crucial to recognize the need for a mental break.

> "THE GREATEST WEAPON AGAINST STRESS IS OUR ABILITY TO CHOOSE ONE THOUGHT OVER ANOTHER."
> -WILLIAM JAMES

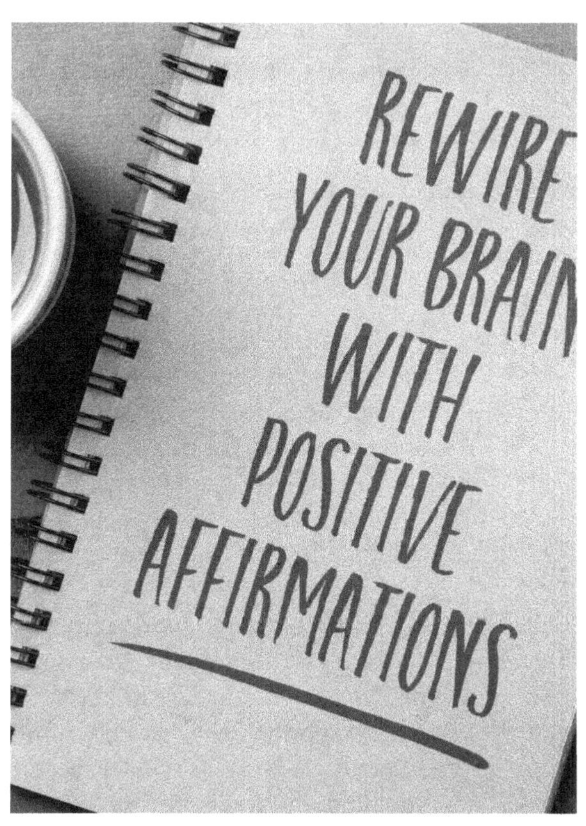

You Feel Overwhelmed and Helpless

In conclusion, if you're experiencing an overwhelming sense of helplessness, and feel incapable of managing your current responsibilities, it may be time for a mental break. Neglecting such an urge could lead to a possible breakdown. By taking a step back and giving yourself some respite, you can better avoid such outcomes.

SIMPLE WAYS TO DECLUTTER YOUR MIND

5 AWESOME TIPS

The accumulation of thoughts in your mind can become overwhelming clutter. It starts innocently enough with reminders to pay bills, complete household chores, take children to practice, and run errands. Over time, this mental clutter builds up, leading to stress and anxiety.

As a result, you may experience chronic headaches, persistent back pain, sleep and appetite disturbances, and heightened anxiety. All of which can be traced back to the stress caused by excessive mind clutter.

If this resonates with you, there are several simple steps you can take to alleviate mental clutter and restore balance to your mind.

>>> STOP FEELING SORRY FOR YOURSELF

The process of decluttering your mind can be challenging, especially since it's easy to fall into negative thought patterns. Negative thoughts tend to be more accessible than positive ones, but if you aim to eliminate the stress and overwhelm from your mind, you must shift your focus towards positivity.

To achieve this, it's crucial to halt any self-pitying, self-disappointment, guilt-ridden, or self-pitying mentality. What has already transpired is irreversible, so accepting it and moving forward is the best solution. Rather than telling yourself you can't accomplish something, find ways to achieve it, or adjust your perspective and goals. It's important to cultivate confidence in yourself and your abilities to transform the clutter in your mind into a positive outlook.

STOP DOUBTING YOUR OWN ABILITIES

In certain aspects, mental clutter accumulates when one lacks the determination or courage to accomplish tasks. It's important not to allow self-doubt to occupy valuable space in your mind. By adopting a positive outlook, building confidence, and recognizing one's capabilities, you can tackle the projects you've been envisioning for an extended period.

DECLUTTER YOUR HOME AND WORKSPACE <<<

To declutter your mind, it's essential to organize and simplify your physical surroundings as well, including your home and workspace. The accumulation of physical clutter can over-stimulate your senses and lead to feelings of stress and overwhelm. A helpful tip is to survey your surroundings and reduce the physical clutter wherever possible. This might include organizing your belongings, decluttering your refrigerator, maintaining a simple decor in your bedroom, and removing any laundry from sight. Similarly, a clutter-free workspace can help you concentrate better on your tasks at hand.

Choose Your Priorities

Achieving a state of zero worry and perfect organization at all times is an unrealistic goal. However, we can begin by prioritizing our responsibilities and determining which ones we can handle ourselves and which ones we should delegate or discard.

As individuals, we are limited in our capacity to manage everything, and some of our concerns may not be our own or lack significance. Therefore, it's essential to establish priorities for our personal life, career, and home obligations.

Our family should be the highest priority, so while it's tempting to extend help to friends, we must acknowledge our limitations. I suggest listing your responsibilities and thoughts and arranging them in order of priority, focusing first on the most important ones.

Write Everything Down

To declutter your mind, it's crucial to alleviate it of any thoughts, concerns, or feelings that may be weighing it down. One method is to put pen to paper and jot down everything that comes to mind. Whether it's a to-do list or a worry about an upcoming event, writing it down can be an effective way to clear your mind.

Additionally, performing a 'big brain dump' by writing down all of your thoughts and feelings in your journal can help to organize and make sense of them. Repeat these practices as needed to maintain a clear and uncluttered mind.

EFFECTIVE WAYS TO KEEP CALM WHEN CONFRONTED WITH STRESSFUL SITUATIONS

To overcome stress in life, it's vital to identify stressors and work towards minimizing their impact. However, it's impossible to control every situation that may trigger stress. Stress is a natural response of the body that can lead to fight or flight response. Therefore, it's essential to learn how to react to stressful situations when they arise and continue living our lives.

Continue reading to discover ways to remain calm and composed even in the face of significant stressors.

Stop Your Body and Thoughts

When confronted with a stressful situation, it's imperative to remember that you have the power to choose your reaction. Your thoughts, emotions, and physical response are within your control. Reacting negatively and impulsively will only exacerbate your stress levels, causing you to feel overwhelmed.

Instead, take a moment to pause and distance yourself from the situation. Allow your thoughts to settle, without overanalyzing or ruminating on the past or future. It's vital to find a peaceful space to regain a sense of calm, whether that's through meditation, mindfulness practices, or physical stillness. This will enable you to approach the situation logically and with a clear mind.

Discover the Power of Positivity

Maintaining a positive outlook can have a significant impact on your mental and emotional well-being, as well as your ability to cope with stress. It's important to note that positivity doesn't equate to a life void of challenges or obstacles. Acknowledging life's imperfections and accepting personal shortcomings are crucial steps towards developing a positive mindset.

Stress is an inevitable aspect of life, and instead of allowing it to consume you mentally and physically, you can choose to remain calm by adopting a positive attitude. This can be achieved by identifying and focusing on positive elements, either by weighing pros and cons or by finding at least one optimistic aspect of the situation. Trust me, there's always something positive to hold onto amidst stress.

Stop with the Assumptions and 'What If' Questions

It's imperative to abstain from making assumptions and indulging in constant what-if scenarios. Doing so only triggers anxiety and stress, which could otherwise be avoidable. To identify the root of your stress, evaluate whether it arises from external factors or your perception of it.

Consider maintaining a journal to log stressful incidents and record the actual situation that occurred rather than the fears or what-if scenarios that may have triggered them. You might find that your anxieties were more severe than the reality of the situation.

During a stressful experience, it's essential to take a step back, remain present, and focus on the facts of the situation. Avoid assuming the worst-case scenario or creating mental images of potential catastrophes. Such practices only contribute to daily stress levels and should be avoided.

Identify YOUR STRESS TRIGGERS

Mantras and Affirmations for Stress

Reducing stress can be achieved through various methods, such as developing healthier habits, maintaining a balanced diet, engaging in physical activity, identifying stressors, and exploring other options. Another effective approach involves incorporating mantras or affirmations into your daily routine, which can be customized to suit your preferences.

While affirmations are designed to inspire and motivate, mantras are sacred phrases that have been utilized for an extended period. Despite their differences, both mantras and affirmations serve the same purpose of promoting positivity and reducing stress levels.

It's crucial to gain a comprehensive understanding of the root cause(s) of your stress. While you may already have a general idea, maintaining a worry or stress journal can provide more clarity and detail on the matter.

Consider using a designated journal to document your stressors. Ensure it includes pertinent details, such as the location, time, date, people involved, and any other relevant information. This approach can aid in pinpointing the underlying causes of your stress.

Jot down elements such as the root cause of your stress, what thought processes were occurring at the time, and the eventual outcome.

Do you detect any recurrent trends? Are there specific factors that contribute to more stress? Is it work or your personal life? Is there someone in your life who is consistently present during stressful situations? These specifics will assist in identifying triggers, enabling you to avoid them in the future.

5 Mantras to Help Reduce Stress

1. "I am calm, I am at peace." This mantra can help you focus on cultivating a sense of inner peace and tranquility, allowing you to let go of stress and anxiety.
2. "This too shall pass." Reminding yourself that difficult times are temporary can help put current stressors into perspective, providing comfort and hope for the future.
3. "I choose to let go of what I cannot control." This mantra encourages acceptance and release of things beyond your control, allowing you to focus your energy on what you can change.
4. "I am grateful for this moment." Focusing on gratitude can shift your perspective and help you appreciate the present moment, reducing stress and promoting a more positive mindset.
5. "I trust in the process of life." Trusting in the natural flow of life and having faith in your own resilience can help alleviate stress and foster a sense of inner peace and balance.

Why Use Mantras and Affirmations?

Primarily, comprehending the underlying reasons that affirmations and mantras mitigate stress is beneficial. These phrases can aid in various aspects of one's life, such as promoting optimism, providing focus and direction, enhancing wellness, and minimizing anxiety. However, these benefits are just the tip of the iceberg when it comes to the potential advantages of using affirmations and mantras.

Outlined next are some of the ways in which affirmations and mantras can help alleviate stress:

Utilizing mantras can be an effective way to manage stress stemming from specific situations in your life. By selecting positive affirmations, you can better cope with these stressors without allowing them to consume you.

Moreover, practicing mantras can boost your confidence and help you move forward. When dealing with significant levels of stress, it's common to experience a loss of confidence and self-esteem. In such circumstances, a confidence boost can be instrumental in helping you regain control of your life.

Affirmations designed to alleviate stress can help achieve a relaxed state of mind, especially during episodes of anxiety or panic attacks. Incorporating such affirmations can prove beneficial in managing stress levels.

Furthermore, positive affirmations have a broader impact as they promote a positive mindset that can help improve various aspects of one's life. This is particularly valuable for individuals dealing with stress and anxiety.

HOW TO USE THEM

Utilizing affirmations is a straightforward process, with various options available to suit your lifestyle, habits, and requirements. Some effective ways to incorporate affirmations into your daily routine include:

Writing them down in a journal or planner: This is a simple way to use affirmations daily, especially if you prefer to have them written down in one place. You can dedicate a section of your journal or write a different one for each day's entry, depending on your needs.

Using different affirmations each day: If you find repeating the same affirmations monotonous, you can choose a different mantra daily, depending on the stressors in your life.

Keeping your go-to affirmations in a convenient place: If you have a few mantras that significantly help you, consider placing them in a spot where you will regularly see them, such as on your bathroom mirror or inside a cabinet you open every day.

Other ways to incorporate affirmations: You can also use affirmations during daily meditation, during mindful practice, or while practicing self-care routines.

Remember, affirmations are a powerful tool for cultivating a positive mindset. Choose ones that resonate with you, practice regularly, and observe the positive impact they have on your life.

GUIDELINES FOR CHOOSING THE BEST ONES

If you're uncertain about how to select affirmations, there are a few principles that may aid in your decision-making process.

First, consider the feelings evoked by the affirmation. Reflect not only on your emotions while reading it but also when verbalizing it. Does it elicit a sense of calm and positivity or increase stress and negative emotions?

Secondly, determine the purpose of the affirmation. An affirmation that you repeat daily and place on your bathroom mirror may differ significantly from one you record in your journal, tailored to a specific goal.

Finally, ensure that the chosen affirmation is calming, positive and relaxing, particularly when it relates to stress management.

Dealing with Involuntary Thoughts: Tips and Tricks

Intrusive thoughts, defined as unwanted thoughts that persistently recur in your mind, can be overwhelming and feel beyond your control. These thoughts can stem from various sources, including stress, anxiety, past regrets, or future fears. The repetitive nature of these thoughts can lead to excessive rumination, stress, and overanalysis, which can significantly impact your mental wellbeing.

While intrusive thoughts can be challenging to manage, they are not entirely uncontrollable. With effective methods, you can learn to manage these thoughts and lessen their impact on your mental health.

What Triggers Intrusive Thoughts?

Intrusive thoughts are often unwelcome and intrusive, occurring without warning. They can take many forms, such as unwanted images, flashbacks of past traumatic experiences, or persistent worries and fears that play out in the mind. These thoughts can be stubborn, and it may feel like the more you try to push them away, the more they persist.

While intrusive thoughts themselves can be a source of stress, they often arise from a state of stress or overwhelm. This can make it difficult to remain calm and positive, and some people may feel embarrassed or ashamed of their thoughts.

If intrusive thoughts are causing significant distress, exacerbating stress levels, or interfering with daily life, it is essential to take action.

When Intrusive Thoughts Become Obsessions

In some cases, intrusive thoughts may be a symptom of an underlying mental health condition, such as anxiety, depression, or obsessive-compulsive disorder (OCD). Seeking treatment from a mental health professional is crucial in such circumstances, as living with the disorder can exacerbate stress levels and worsen symptoms.

For those with OCD, intrusive thoughts can become obsessive, leading to an inability to stop thinking about them and sometimes acting on them. If intrusive thoughts are causing significant disruption to daily life, the following tips may be helpful in managing them.

PRACTICE MINDFULNESS

Practicing mindfulness can be transformative, particularly in dealing with persistent thoughts that may feel overwhelming. Mindfulness emphasizes comprehending the thoughts without attempting to eliminate them. By accepting the present moment's reality, it becomes easier to avoid excessive rumination on past events or future possibilities that may never come to fruition.

SWITCH YOUR THOUGHTS

While it may not be possible to eradicate intrusive thoughts merely by wishing them away, it's often helpful to distract your mind, even if only for a short duration. These brief intermissions can provide some relief from the associated stress. Although it may seem insignificant, it's a constructive step that can gradually lead to longer periods of distraction, ultimately alleviating the distress caused by these unwelcome thoughts.

WRITE IT DOWN

When one has an abundance of thoughts occupying their mind, a helpful technique is performing a "brain dump" into a personal journal. This approach is effective for both thoughts one wishes to contemplate, as well as those that are unwanted. Furthermore, a journal provides a confidential and private outlet, allowing individuals to express their innermost thoughts without fear of judgment or disclosure to others.

TALK TO SOMEONE

It's highly recommended to express your feelings to someone trustworthy, regardless of whether you divulge the specifics of your intrusive thoughts or just seek a healthy distraction. Consider reaching out to a family member or friend through a phone call or text, or even arranging a coffee date. Such interactions can provide a temporary respite from your intrusive thoughts.

EFFORTLESS WAYS TO MANAGE UNCONTROLLABLE THOUGHTS

In the event that you are still struggling to manage your intrusive thoughts, there are additional strategies you can implement to mitigate them. Doing so will enable you to regulate your stress levels and avoid feeling overwhelmed. Here are some more tips to help with intrusive thoughts:

Practicing mindfulness can aid in accepting these thoughts and then moving beyond them. By reaching a state of acceptance, rather than attempting to eliminate the thoughts, you can acknowledge them and attempt to release their hold over you.

UNDERSTAND WHY THE THOUGHTS ARE THERE TO BEGIN WITH.

Sometimes your uncontrollable thoughts are trying to tell you something, similar to how a dream isn't realistic, but it is sending you a message or explains what your subconscious is going through.

It's important to pay attention to these thoughts and try to understand what they're trying to communicate. They could be a reflection of underlying fears, anxieties, or desires that you haven't fully acknowledged or dealt with yet. Acknowledging and processing these thoughts can help you gain a better understanding of yourself and your emotions. It's also important to remember that everyone experiences intrusive or uncontrollable thoughts at some point in their lives, and there's no need to feel ashamed or embarrassed about them. With self-awareness and practice, you can learn to manage and cope with these thoughts in a healthy way.

STOP TRYING TO WILL THEM AWAY.

This isn't going to work, and may even cause you to focus more on them. Think about it like a craving. If you have a craving for something, the more you try to get rid of the craving, the more you want it. But if you have just one of whatever you're craving, it eventually goes away.

The same goes for negative thoughts or emotions towards someone. The more you try to push them away or ignore them, the stronger they become. Instead, try to acknowledge those feelings and understand where they are coming from. Once you have done that, try to shift your focus towards positive thoughts and actions. It could be something as simple as thinking of a happy memory or doing something you enjoy. Over time, you may find that those negative feelings towards the person dissipate and you are able to move on. Remember, it takes time and effort to change your mindset, but it is possible and worth it in the end.

Strategies for Practicing Mindfulness When Overwhelmed.

If you find yourself struggling to manage your daily responsibilities, worries, and stress, it's possible that you're experiencing feelings of being overwhelmed. While this might appear to be commonplace, it can have adverse effects on both your mental and physical well-being. Fortunately, there are strategies to alleviate these sentiments, starting with mindfulness practices.

Mindfulness has become a ubiquitous topic due to its numerous benefits. Essentially, it refers to the practice of being present and aware of one's thoughts. It's a simple technique to adopt and can significantly enhance one's overall mindset. Mindfulness has been shown to alleviate feelings of stress and overwhelm, among other benefits.

What is Mindfulness?

Mindfulness has become a prevalent topic of discussion, particularly concerning personal growth, mental wellness, and stress reduction. Practicing mindfulness can be advantageous in various stress-inducing scenarios, including burnout and feelings of overwhelm.

Mindfulness is a mental state characterized by heightened awareness of one's thoughts and intentions, leading to a place of acceptance and present living. It encompasses a broad spectrum of practices, but at its core, it is about acknowledging and being present in the current moment. Whether it is dealing with stress, enjoying a meal, or working on a craft project, being mindful can help individuals derive greater value from their experiences.

Living in the Present

The initial step of mindfulness is to reside in the present moment, an approach that can prove beneficial to individuals grappling with the pressures of stress in their lives. Overwhelm can result in difficulty focusing on important elements of one's life. The mind becomes cluttered, making it feel insurmountable to manage everything effectively.

This is where mindfulness can be particularly useful. Mindfulness provides the ability to live in the present moment, where attention is wholly devoted to the current instant. What is critical right now? Not next week, next month, or next year. Not contemplating past events. JUST concentrate on the present moment. This strategy can help to streamline thoughts and allow individuals to prioritize their actions more effectively.

MINDFUL EXERCISES AND TECHNIQUES

Mindfulness can be a straightforward process, based on its intended use and the context in which it is being applied. The fundamental technique involves being present and noting down your thoughts, emotions, and actions at that moment. For instance, if you're seeking to practice mindfulness during your meals, you could maintain a journal and document how you feel while consuming your food. Does it provide nourishment? Are you enjoying the flavors? Are you content with your choices? This method can be conducive to intuitive eating as well.

If you're new to mindfulness or struggling to remain present, there are various exercises you can try. The following are some recommended exercises to get started:

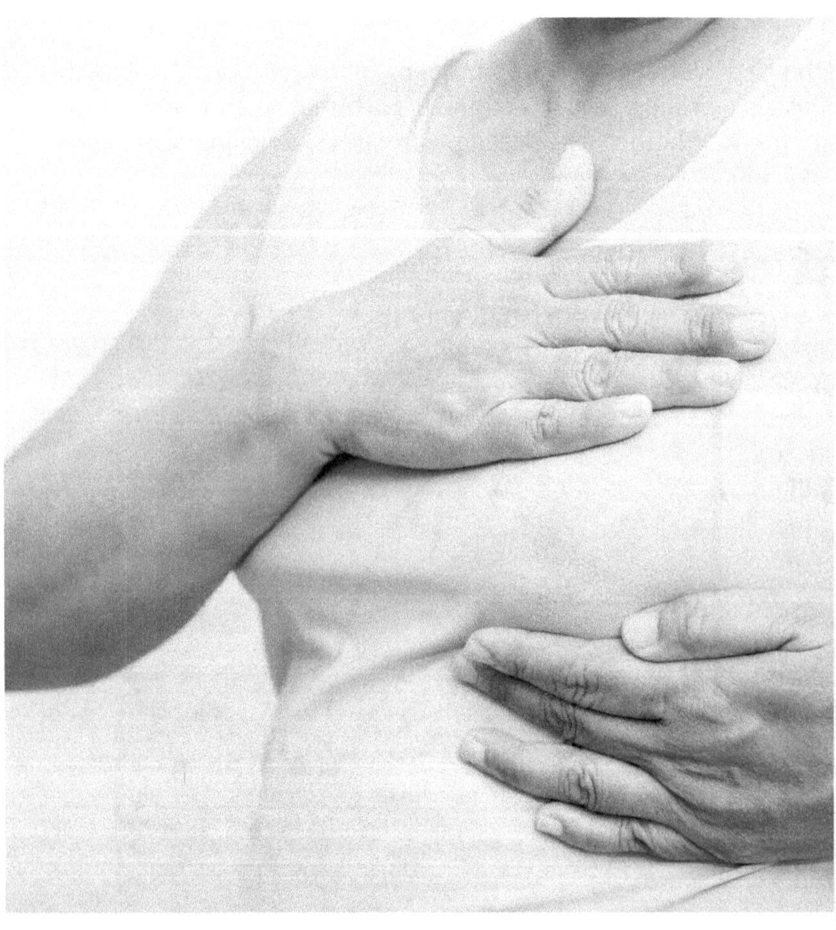

BODY SCAN

The initial technique is an excellent practice for both mindfulness and meditation. It involves a body scan exercise in which you mentally survey each part of your body, secluding one section at a time. This approach encourages mindfulness by fixing your awareness on every part of your body and how it feels at the moment, leading to a relaxed, meditative state.

Rather than dwelling on any worries, the focus is directed towards specific body parts, such as the scalp, ears, chest, stomach, arms, legs, hands, or feet. Take time to pay attention to each body part separately, concentrating on it mindfully.

BREATHING

An alternative technique to cultivate mindfulness is through a breathing exercise. Focusing solely on your breath can induce a meditative state, detaching your mind from the past or future. The steps are uncomplicated: designate a peaceful area where you won't be interrupted. Take a deep inhale, followed by a slow exhale. As you breathe, attempt to hold each breath for a few seconds, allowing your mind and body to relax.

USE YOUR SENSES

The last mindful exercise you can try out is where you try to use all of your senses in this moment. For example, what do you smell? Do you feel anything near you? If you're eating or drinking, what do you taste? Use all 5 of your senses for this practice.

This exercise can be extremely helpful in bringing you back to the present moment and grounding you. It's easy to get lost in thoughts about the past or worries about the future, but by focusing on your senses, you can become more aware of your surroundings and less caught up in your thoughts. This can be especially useful if you're feeling anxious or stressed, as it can help calm your mind and bring you back to a more relaxed state. So next time you're feeling overwhelmed, take a moment to pause and use your senses to bring yourself back to the present moment.

CHAPTER 4 EXPLORES THE SIGNIFICANCE OF JOURNALING AS A MEANS OF SELF-CARE

The Significance of Self-Care in: Alleviating Stress

The suggestions for alleviating stress can vary considerably, depending on the source, as there are numerous remedies to choose from. Nevertheless, one common recommendation is to prioritize self-care, which you may hear from almost anyone. It's crucial to be attentive to your individual needs, prioritize personal well-being, and identify when a little self-compassion is necessary. Here are some reasons why self-care plays a vital role in stress management.

Firstly, self-care helps you to create a balance between life's demands and personal needs. It's easy to get carried away with responsibilities such as work, family, and other obligations, and forget to take a break. However, taking time for yourself to relax and recharge is essential to maintain optimal functioning. Self-care activities such as meditation, yoga, or reading can help you to slow down and reduce stress levels.

Secondly, prioritizing self-care helps to boost your mood and increase your overall well-being. Engaging in activities that bring you joy and fulfillment can elevate your mood and improve your mental health. Self-care can also help to reduce anxiety and depression symptoms, which are often associated with high-stress levels.

Lastly, self-care can help you to build resilience and cope with stressors better. When you prioritize your well-being, you become better equipped to handle life's challenges. You're better able to identify your triggers and develop healthy coping mechanisms to manage stressors effectively.

In summary, self-care is an integral component of stress management. By prioritizing your well-being, you can create balance, boost your mood, and build resilience to cope with stressors. So take some time for yourself, and incorporate self-care activities into your daily routine.

WHAT PEOPLE GET WRONG ABOUT SELF-CARE

Self-care encompasses a diverse range of activities and tasks, some of which may not typically be associated with it. At its core, self-care involves dedicating time to nurture oneself without external pressures or expectations. While some people may associate self-care with reading a book or indulging in a bubble bath, the practice extends beyond these activities. Examples of self-care include socializing with friends, exercising or taking a walk, consuming a favorite meal, or spending time with a pet. It's crucial to acknowledge that self-care is not a selfish act. Rather, it's an intentional commitment to one's well-being that everyone should prioritize.

WHY YOU SHOULD TURN TO SELF-CARE FIRST!

In times of heightened stress and anxiety, it's essential to take a mental break. Incorporating more self-care practices into your routine can be an effective strategy to manage daily stress and enhance your overall well-being. While stress may not always be a result of lacking self-care, it's still a valuable tool to help you achieve a relaxed mind and body, providing the opportunity to refocus your thoughts.

By taking a step back and indulging in self-care, you can prevent yourself from mindlessly attempting to stay busy and tackling tasks without proper intention. This approach allows you to take deliberate action towards your goals, rather than merely trying to keep occupied. It's a common pitfall that many individuals encounter when facing stressful situations.

Start with Daily Activities for Your Health and Wellbeing

If you're unsure about the concept of self-care or how to begin implementing it, it's useful to start with a few simple daily activities. Consider actions that positively impact your physical or mental wellbeing, decrease stress levels, and facilitate relaxation. Here are a few daily activities that can be considered self-care:

- Improving the quality of your sleep.
- Engaging in activities that help you relax.
- Journaling or using a planner to organize your thoughts.
- Setting aside quiet time for reading.
- Drinking more water to stay hydrated.
- Incorporating healthier foods into your diet.
- Regularly exercising to maintain physical fitness.

Tap into Your Senses

One effective approach to cultivate mindfulness and relieve stress is by engaging in activities that stimulate your senses. Consider the various senses, such as taste, touch, hearing, smell, and sight, and how to incorporate them into your routine. Some simple yet effective examples include:

- Listening to calming music, the sound of rain, or running water.
- Taking a bubble bath, feeling the warm water, and enjoying the fragrance of bubbles.
- Getting a massage to relax your muscles.
- Watching the flames of a fire in your living room to create a serene atmosphere.
- Wrapping yourself in a soft blanket to feel cozy and comfortable.

Incorporating these simple activities into your self-care routine can help you tap into your senses and develop mindfulness, ultimately reducing your stress levels.

Additional Self-Care Activities to Alleviate Stress.

Self-care activities extend beyond the fundamental practices and encompass any endeavors that offer a sense of happiness and relaxation. Consider options that can be pursued both at home and outside, such as embarking on a road trip or vacation, enjoying coffee with a friend, a date night with a significant other, or attending regular art classes.

It's important to note that self-care is subjective, and its effectiveness is measured by the extent to which it improves your mental and physical well-being. Prioritizing self-care activities can be instrumental in reducing overall stress and anxiety.

Writing it Out:
Journaling for Stress, Burnout, and Overwhelm

Individuals who frequently encounter stressful situations are acutely aware of the detrimental effects it can have on their mental, emotional, and physical well-being. The repercussions of stress can result in a sense of being overwhelmed, burnout, and difficulties in both professional and personal relationships.

If you identify with these challenges, it's critical to address them and find healthy coping mechanisms to manage stress. Writing is an effective approach that can yield numerous benefits beyond stress relief.

Here are some ways to incorporate writing as a tool to help manage stress and reclaim control of your life.

The Advantages of Journaling as a Stress Reliever

Journaling is an invaluable tool for tackling stress. It offers numerous benefits, including providing an outlet for a "brain dump" and aiding in identifying the root cause of stress. Should you notice that your stress is intermittent, reviewing previous entries in your stress journal can help you identify patterns and pinpoint your primary stress triggers.

Moreover, journaling provides a safe space to express your worries and frustrations without the fear of overburdening others.

Try a Brain Dump

One effective technique to alleviate stress and declutter the mind is the brain dump. It involves jotting down all your thoughts, ideas, concerns, and worries onto paper. Engaging in stream-of-consciousness journaling allows you to write whatever comes to mind without worrying about organizing your thoughts. As a result, you might discover worries that you didn't even realize you had. This process aids in finding clarity in your thoughts and decluttering the mind. Keep writing until you feel that all significant thoughts have been expressed on the paper.

Have a Worry or Stress Journal

Although you can journal in any type of notebook, having a dedicated worry journal can be an effective way to manage stress. This type of journal is specifically utilized to record your thoughts when you're feeling overwhelmed or attempting to navigate a challenging situation. Maintaining a worry journal can help you maintain organized thoughts and provide an easy way to locate specific entries when needed.

Talk About Your Anxiety And Depression

Expressing your thoughts and emotions regarding your anxiety or depression is crucial. You can also document other mental health issues you're encountering, including the ways in which your depression or anxiety is influenced. It's beneficial to maintain these entries alongside your anxiety or worry journal, as they often overlap.

If you're struggling with clinical depression, you're aware that depressive episodes tend to be cyclical. Nevertheless, you may not recognize the correlation between depression and stress or comprehend all your triggers until you begin chronicling your experiences in your journal.

Track Your Different Triggers

Maintaining a journal for stress, burnout, and overwhelm is advantageous in tracking triggers that lead to these experiences. It's essential to identify the root cause of these emotions, not just the timing. By being detailed in each entry, you'll begin to discern recurring patterns. For instance, triggers might emerge at the same time each week, near payday, or within personal relationships.

Write in the Journal Throughout the Day

When using journaling as a tool to cope with stress and overwhelm, consider writing at varying times throughout the day. While morning and nighttime journaling can be beneficial, it might be necessary to have your journal readily available during the day, particularly if you encounter stressful situations.

In the event of a stressful occurrence during the day, having your journal at arm's reach allows you to document your thoughts and feelings and continue with your day.

Effective Techniques to Reduce Daily Anxiety.

It's common to encounter work-related stress due to the inherent demands of the job. Managing projects, supervising teams, and fulfilling work expectations can be challenging. Unforeseen events can also add to the stress levels.

While it may not be possible to avoid all stressors, there are methods to alleviate stress while continuing to manage work and other responsibilities.

Improve Your Work Relationships

A lot of the stress you experience at work can be relieved just by working harder on your work relationships and friendships. When everyone gets along, people tend to support each other, help each other, and work together much more efficiently. Even if your work stress isn't directly related to the people you work with, this can still be really beneficial for you.

Here are some tips for working on your work relationships:

- Initiate a conversation with a colleague you haven't spoken to before or someone new to the organization. A simple introduction and some casual questions can go a long way in building a connection.
- Invite a colleague, whether a close friend or someone you don't know well, to join you for lunch. This provides an opportunity to develop a stronger relationship outside of work tasks.
- Offer assistance to a colleague who could use help with a challenging project or task. Being supportive and helpful conveys a sense of teamwork and camaraderie.

Find Out What Your Stressors Are

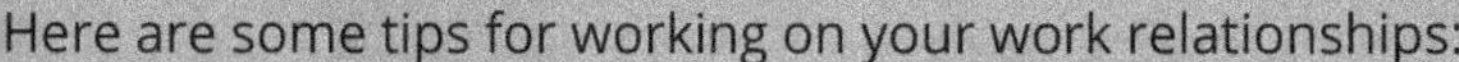

To effectively overcome work-related stress, it's crucial to identify the primary stressors. These could be anything from the vending machine if you're concerned about weight gain, to an overwhelming workload, or even interpersonal conflicts within the workplace.

As stressors vary from person to person, it's essential to examine your own situation. For a week, maintain a journal or notebook, and record each instance of feeling stressed, including what was happening at the time, your thoughts, and the situation's specifics. These details, such as the timing of the event, whether it was during lunch break or after speaking to a colleague, or if a client or customer was involved, can help pinpoint the root cause of your stress.

Give Yourself Time to Recharge

Regardless of your profession, whether it be in an office setting, outdoors, or at home, it's essential to carve out time to recharge. Identify what causes you the most stress and create distance from it, even if it's just a little bit each day.

Working from home can be a unique challenge, as there's often an expectation to be working at all times. To recharge, it's necessary to shut down your laptop, turn off your phone, and intentionally shift your mindset to taking a break or concluding work for the day. It's crucial to recognize the difference between working and taking time for yourself.

Have a Flexible Schedule

Attempting to micro-manage and meticulously plan every minute of your day can result in burnout and fatigue. Even if the intent is to enhance productivity, the stress of a rigid schedule can be overwhelming.

While scheduling and planning are beneficial, it's critical to avoid being overly strict with your itinerary. A flexible schedule with alternatives for unexpected situations allows for a more balanced approach that considers self-care and the need for occasional downtime.

HERE ARE SIX TIPS TO COMBAT BURNOUT AND OVERWHELMING FEELINGS:

Enduring high levels of stress can lead to burnout or feeling overwhelmed. Overwhelm is a result of prolonged exposure to stress, causing one to feel inundated with thoughts and responsibilities. Burnout, on the other hand, occurs when an individual becomes emotionally and physically exhausted, leading to a decline in motivation, productivity, and energy levels.

To overcome burnout and overwhelm, consider implementing the following tips and strategies.

01. A HEALTHY BODY MEANS A HEALTHY MIND

The path towards overcoming burnout, stress, and feeling overwhelmed begins with prioritizing your physical health. Not only can stress manifest in physical ailments, but a healthy diet and exercise routine can provide a host of benefits.

A healthy mind necessitates a healthy body, which can be achieved through consuming a balanced diet comprising of fruits, vegetables, lean protein, and whole grains. Regular exercise and staying hydrated by drinking enough water are also crucial.

Incorporating these modest changes can significantly boost your physical health, which, in turn, positively impacts your mental well-being.

02. STOP FOCUSING ON TIME

Time seems to be the overarching theme in our lives. We strive to balance our family and work obligations, frequently checking the clock during the workday, and attempting to leave the house with ample time. The emphasis on time management, including feeling that it's wasted or running out, can lead to inordinate stress and anxiety.

While time is undoubtedly relevant for certain aspects of our lives, such as punctuality for appointments, it's crucial not to allow it to consume us entirely. Maintaining a balanced perspective on time can help alleviate unnecessary stress and promote a healthier mindset.

03. STAY MINDFUL OF POSITIVE CHANGES AND A BETTER OUTLOOK

When experiencing severe burnout, conventional stress-relieving techniques may not be effective. At this stage, completing even the most basic tasks can be a challenge, compounded by feelings of stress and overwhelm.

Rather than overwhelming yourself with high expectations, consider starting small. One effective method is practicing mindfulness for a brief moment each day. During this moment, take a few minutes to redirect negative energy to positive energy.

For instance, after a meeting that caused stress and tension, take five minutes to practice mindfulness and focus on something positive. This could be gratitude for securing a job you worked hard for, appreciation for family and friends, or simply acknowledging the fact that the stressful situation has passed and you were able to overcome it.

04. DON'T WORK THROUGH LUNCH

It's essential to acknowledge that working tirelessly is not an effective approach to overcoming burnout. A much-needed break is necessary to enable your body and mind to rest and rejuvenate. Continuously working throughout the week will leave you devoid of energy to enjoy your weekend.

To start, consider taking proper lunch breaks by avoiding eating at your desk or talking on the phone while consuming your meal outside the office. Disconnect from work, relish in your meal, and take the time to relax. Once your break is over, you can return to your work with renewed energy and focus.

05. FIND WHAT GIVES YOU POSITIVE ENERGY

Find a source of positivity and happiness in your daily routine. This will cultivate a more optimistic outlook and potentially alleviate some of the stress and anxiety you may be experiencing.

This source will be personal and unique to your individual circumstances, such as your home, job, relationships, achieving personal goals, improving physical health, or any other aspect that brings joy to your life. The possibilities are limitless.

06. START SAYING NO

If you are someone who is frequently relied upon for assistance, it's important to recognize that you cannot be everything to everyone. It's perfectly acceptable to decline invites, whether it's hosting a get-together, going out on your sole night off, or taking on an additional work project.

Learning to say no when you're already swamped with your own tasks and obligations is essential.

CHAPTER 5
DISCOVER ADDITIONAL NATURAL STRESS RELIEF REMEDIES

RELIEVING STRESS THROUGH ESSENTIAL OILS

UNDERSTANDING DIFFERENT TYPES OF STRESS AND HOW ESSENTIAL OILS CAN HELP RELIEVE THEM

Stress can manifest in diverse ways and is generally classified into three main types: acute stress, chronic stress, and episodic stress. Acute stress is brief and typically short-lived, whereas chronic stress is recurrent and prolonged. Episodic stress is self-inflicted and may occur in cycles. Regardless of the stress type, natural remedies are often sought to alleviate its effects. Essential oils, derived from herbs, can be beneficial in reducing stress levels and promoting relaxation.

As you may know, essential oils are oils derived from various parts of plants, herbs, and flowers. These oils can be extracted from leaves, flower petals, stems, and other plant parts.

The extraction process for each oil varies, with lavender oil, for instance, extracted differently than lemon essential oil.

Essential oils have been used for centuries for their therapeutic properties. They can be used in a variety of ways such as aromatherapy, massage, and even in household cleaning products. Essential oils are also believed to have a positive effect on mental health, with some oils being used to reduce stress and anxiety, while others are used to promote relaxation and better sleep. When used responsibly, essential oils can be a great addition to one's self-care routine.

NEVER USED ESSENTIAL OILS?

If you're new to the world of essential oils, it's crucial to be aware of some fundamental tips, tricks, and facts before beginning to use them for stress relief:

- There are various ways to use essential oils, and each oil's optimal use depends on individual preference and intended benefits. For instance, lavender oil is excellent for sunburns and skin irritations and can be applied directly to the skin. Other usages for oils include diffusing, adding to bathwater, and incorporating into body and skincare products.
- Diluting essential oils is necessary before applying them to the skin. Pure essential oils are potent and too strong to be applied directly to the skin. Thus, they should be diluted with a carrier oil such as olive oil, grapeseed oil, or jojoba oil.
- Each essential oil boasts multiple health benefits beyond stress relief, ranging from chronic pain management to anxiety and depression reduction and soothing itchy skin.
- When purchasing essential oils, ensure that you buy "pure" essential oils and avoid fragrance oils. Carefully inspect the label and product description, whether shopping online or in person, and avoid any product labeled as "fragrance." Choose only those labeled as 100% pure essential oil.

THE BEST ESSENTIAL OILS FOR STRESS RELIEF

If you are interested in using essential oils to help relieve your stress, here are some of the best ones:

Lavender – Lavender is definitely one of the most popular essential oils in general, but can also be amazing for stress, improving your sleep, and reducing anxiety. Lavender is very calming and soothing, helping to relax you, whether you are dealing with a lot of stress in your life, or just want to wind down after a long day.

Frankincense – Frankincense, like all essential oils, has many health benefits. It can be good for reducing inflammation in the body, relieving chronic pain, and yes, helping with stress. It has been used in many essential oil blends aiming at helping with stress and anxiety.

Ylang Ylang – When you look at different essential oils and blends that are recommended for stress and anxiety, you will probably see ylang ylang each and every time. This essential oil really helps to calm and relax your nervous system, which can help with the heightened levels of stress you are experiencing.

Lemon – Lemon is great because it not only helps with stress and anxiety thanks to the light sedative qualities it has, but it can be great for waking you up and helping with fatigue. For this reason, it is a great essential oil to use in the morning if you wake up with anxiety, but you also want to be more alert to take on the day.

Chamomile – This one is likely not surprising, since chamomile tea is often recommended for relaxation and to promote better sleep. Try a little chamomile essential oil or go the traditional route and have the tea to reduce your stress levels.

The Healing Power of

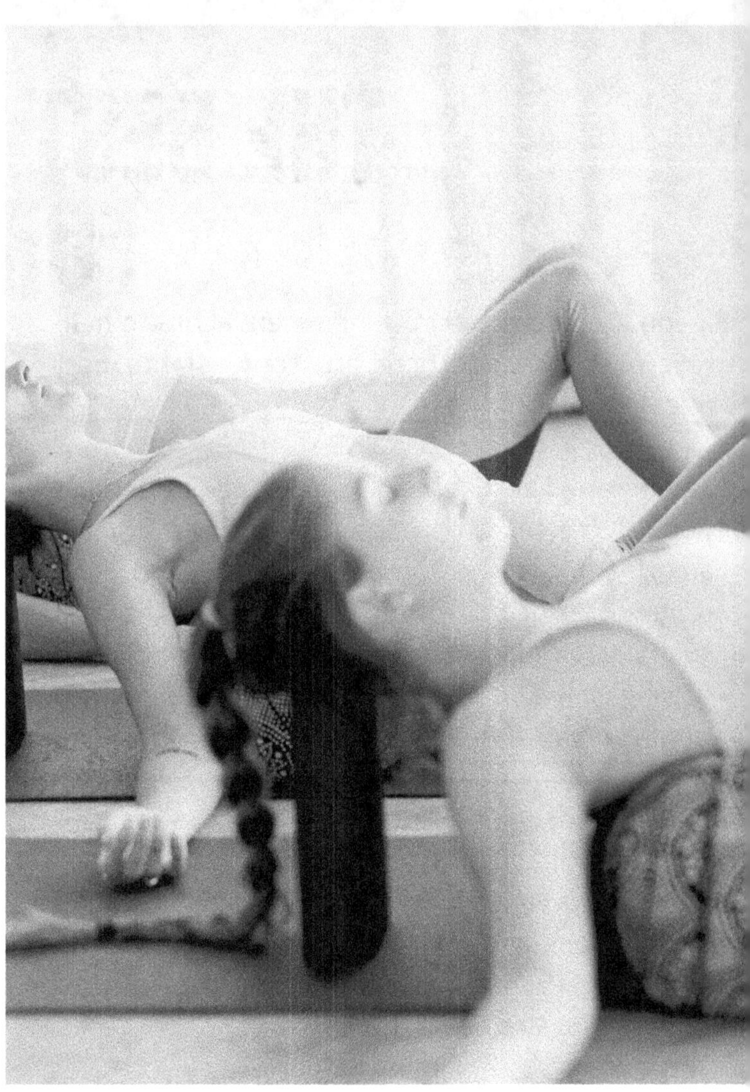

Yoga offers numerous health benefits, with multiple styles to choose from, such as hatha yoga, hot yoga, and restorative yoga, among others. Each style has unique qualities, yet many of the same benefits.

Restorative yoga is a gentle approach to the practice, which focuses on promoting wellness, healing both the body and mind, and integrating basic stretches that stimulate the body's natural ability to repair. Additionally, it is an excellent method for stress relief.

Restorative Yoga for Stress Relief

While most yoga practice can aid in stress relief, restorative yoga provides several additional benefits towards this end. Primarily, restorative yoga is a more deliberate and gentle form of yoga, emphasizing the extended holding of each pose, which allows for greater flexibility and strength-building. This approach enables you to adjust and stretch your body through each pose, while also providing an opportunity to relax and breathe deeply. Furthermore, restorative yoga classes are typically conducted in a serene environment, further promoting relaxation and tranquility, making it an ideal form of yoga for those seeking stress relief.

In addition to physical benefits, restorative yoga also has a positive effect on mental and emotional well-being. The slow and intentional movements, combined with deep breathing, can help calm the mind and reduce anxiety. As you hold each pose, you are encouraged to focus on your breath and let go of any thoughts or worries. This mindful practice can also improve sleep quality and overall mood. It's important to note that restorative yoga is accessible to people of all ages and fitness levels. The use of props such as blankets, blocks, and bolsters make poses more comfortable and can be adjusted to accommodate any physical limitations. Overall, restorative yoga is a gentle and effective way to reduce stress and promote relaxation in both the body and mind.

Why Props Are Used in Restorative Yoga

One of the significant differences between restorative yoga and other yoga practices is the frequent use of props. This gentle form of yoga is designed to induce relaxation, and the props serve to support the body, allowing for proper form and longer hold times of each pose. This extended duration of each position is what makes it "restorative" and beneficial for both the mind and body.

In a class setting, instructors typically provide the necessary props. However, if practicing at home, it's advisable to invest in yoga blocks and bolsters. In the absence of these, rolled-up towels or small blankets can also serve as adequate substitutes.

TOP YOGA POSES TO ALLEVIATE STRESS.

Although numerous yoga asanas utilized in restorative yoga are beneficial for stress relief, certain poses are more suitable for beginners. If you're grappling with stress and anxiety, consider attempting some of these entry-level poses:

CHILD POSE

When initiating a yoga routine, it's wise to commence with a straightforward posture that allows for an easy and gentle stretch, such as the child's pose. If you already partake in other workouts, such as strength training or Pilates, it's possible that you are familiar with this pose as it's a common post-workout stretch. To execute the child's pose, begin on your knees with the top of your feet and shins resting on the ground. Maintain your knees at shoulder-width apart, then proceed to bend your body forward until your head and shoulders are between your knees. Bend forward as much as you're comfortable with, ensuring that your arms are stretched out in front of you. The goal is to achieve a satisfying stretch without any discomfort or pain.

TWIST WITH A BOLSTER

This is one of the restorative yoga poses that uses a prop – or a bolster in this case. This is similar in shape and size to a rolled-up blanket, so that can be used in its place if you don't have the bolster. The twist is amazing for stretching your entire body, and allowing blood to flow through the twist, which can also help you to relax and start relieving stress. Sit down on your mat with the bolster in front of you. You want one of your hips to be at the shorter end of the bolster, with your feet at the opposite side – so, if you are using your left hip, then your feet will be at the right side, and vice versa. Allow the twist to lengthen your spine and hold for as long as you can before exhaling.

LEGS UP THE WALL

Lastly, you can try the legs up the wall yoga pose, another classic pose that is great for beginners. All you need to do is find a wall in your home or the yoga studio that you will be able to lean your body against. You will be laying with your back and buttocks on the ground, with your legs straight up in front of you, on the wall. An easy way to get into this position is put one hip on the wall, lay down flat, then swing your legs around to go up the wall.

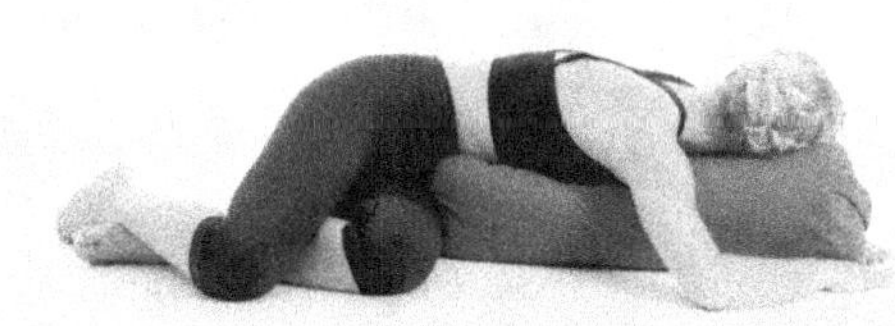

Below are six techniques to unwind when feeling overwhelmed.

If you're experiencing a sense of overwhelming pressure due to your daily responsibilities, it can negatively impact your mental health and overall well-being. This feeling tends to amplify and may exacerbate symptoms of anxiety and depression. However, before you allow yourself to succumb to overwhelming stress, consider incorporating some of these relaxation tips to alleviate stress and promote a sense of calm.

Start a Worry Journal

During times of overwhelming stress, our minds are often filled with a plethora of thoughts, concerns, fears, and regrets. It can be challenging to sort through these emotions, but writing them out can be an effective solution.

Creating a worry journal is an excellent method to pen down all of your worrisome thoughts. Identify the specific events or situations that are causing you the most stress and jot them down in as much detail as you wish. Don't be concerned about grammar or structure; the objective is to let your thoughts flow freely.

The act of writing out your worries will allow you to identify the root cause of your stress and provide a sense of clarity. Start your worry journal today and see how it can aid in managing your feelings of being overwhelmed.

Complete Something You Never Finished

When feeling overwhelmed, an effective way to alleviate stress is by revisiting a task or project you began but never finished. This can be anything, regardless of its scale or relevance to your current objectives.

The reason behind this strategy is that it provides a sense of accomplishment and fulfillment when you complete something. It could be as simple as finishing a home project or something more significant like accomplishing a long-term goal. In either case, the satisfaction of completing a task can be a powerful tool in reducing stress and alleviating feelings of overwhelm.

Wander and Visualize What You Want

Visualization is very powerful, almost magical. When you can see something you want to be, accomplish, or get done, it gives you inspiration and motivation. IT allows you to work hard toward your goals, and actually visualize what the process is like.

But it doesn't have to be only practical. Sometimes what you need the most is to dream. Allow your imagination to be creative and open-minded, dream up something you would love to have in your life, whether it is realistic or not.

Just take a few minutes a day to really visualize this dream, and go as far with it as you need to. When you're done, you will feel calmer and more relaxed, and ready to take on the day.

Develop Healthy Sleep Routines

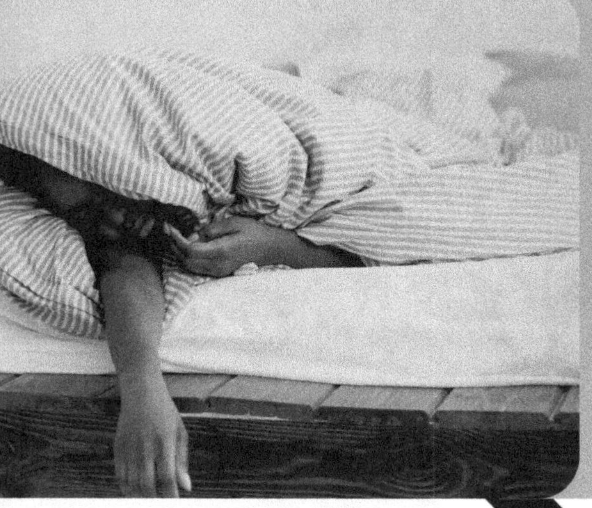

It's imperative to acknowledge the significance of sleep for everyone, including you. No matter your current state of stress or overwhelm, prioritizing rest is crucial for your overall well-being. Quality sleep is vital for preserving memories, gaining focus and energy, and navigating each day with clarity.

If you're experiencing inadequate sleep, consider reviewing your sleep routine. Perhaps you may need to adjust your bedtime or address any issues with pre-sleep cellphone usage. By modifying your routine, you can achieve the much-needed rest that your body and mind require.

Find Your Own Priorities

Determining what holds highest priority in your life is an essential step in managing stress and feelings of being overwhelmed. This is equally applicable to both personal and professional domains. Practicing self-care and alleviating stress involves recognizing the importance of prioritizing oneself.

In the event that a project or goal no longer brings joy and seems to have lost its significance, it may be time to let it go. If it is no longer a priority, there is no reason for it to cause undue stress.

Start a Morning Routine

Establishing a morning routine can significantly contribute to one's success by providing a positive start to the day, avoiding negative attitudes when the alarm goes off, and carving out time for self-care.

Design a morning routine that benefits both your physical and mental well-being. Some suggested activities include practicing yoga, drinking a glass of water, journaling or planning, meditating, or engaging in mindfulness exercises. Although there are no hard and fast rules for a morning routine, ensure that it is tailored to your needs and helps you feel energized and prepared to tackle the day ahead.

WHY SUNDAY SHOULD BE A DAY OF REST

For many individuals who work during the week, weekends are typically filled with additional responsibilities such as workouts, family time, trips, home improvement, cleaning, and other errands.

Although it's necessary to make the most of the days when work responsibilities are minimal, attempting to accomplish too much throughout the week can lead to stressful situations.
To mitigate this, it's essential to consider utilizing Sunday as a day of rest each week, enabling one to adjust their schedule accordingly.

LEAVE YOUR WORK FOR THE WORK WEEK

If you find yourself constantly worrying about work, even during your off hours, you may be exacerbating the stress and strain in your life. This is a common precursor to burnout since you are essentially working around the clock, regardless of whether you're in the office, interacting with clients, answering emails, or simply unable to stop thinking about work.

It's best to concentrate on work only while you're on the clock. Whether you work from home and require a distinct workspace or work outside and leave work-related matters at the office, it's critical to establish boundaries between your work and home life. If you happen to work remotely from home, it's beneficial to have a designated workspace. This approach facilitates a shift in mindset from professional to personal responsibilities. With a dedicated workspace, it's easier to differentiate between work and non-work hours, thereby preventing any unwarranted distractions from seeping into your personal time.

SCHEDULING TOO MUCH OVER THE WEEKEND

One common error when failing to designate proper rest days is overloading your weekend with tasks. While weekends are ideal for completing chores, socializing with friends, and running errands, it's crucial to avoid dedicating the whole weekend to these activities. Otherwise, you may find yourself still fatigued by Monday morning, feeling deprived of personal time.

It's crucial to strike a balance between completing tasks and ensuring you have adequate time to recharge. It may be helpful to schedule time for self-care, such as getting enough rest, and treating it as an appointment you cannot miss.

TAKE A REST FROM EVERYTHING ON SUNDAY

To strike a balance between work and personal life, consider designating Saturday as your sixth day of the week for work or other responsibilities, then keep Sunday solely for yourself. It's important to dedicate Sunday to rest and leisure, rather than filling it up with errands, household chores, or work-related tasks. While it's understandable to want to maximize weekends for productivity, scheduling most of your tasks for Saturday frees up Sunday for personal endeavors.

This doesn't imply that you should spend the whole day idle. Instead, use Sunday to engage in activities of your choice, such as spending quality time with family, shopping, catching up on rest, baking treats, or engaging in hobbies at home.

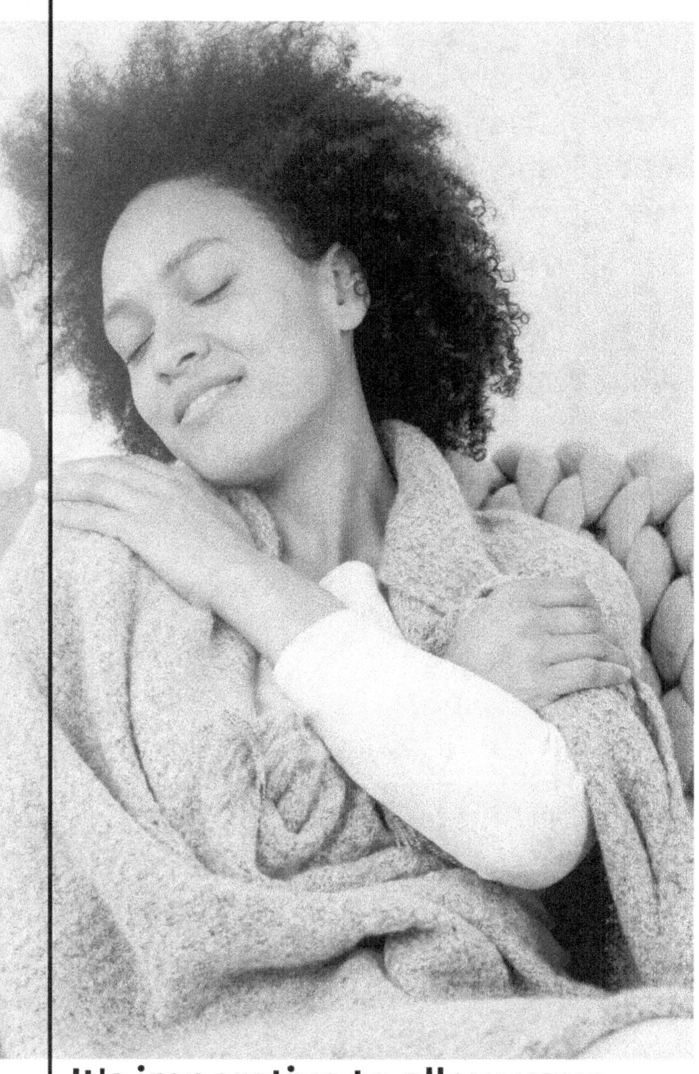

It's imperative to allow your mind and body sufficient rest.

It's imperative to acknowledge that both your mind and body require adequate rest. Even if your idea of unwinding on Sundays involves working from the comfort of your couch, it qualifies as working. Avoid falling into this habit! It's essential to carve out a day or at least half a day a week that requires no work, chores, or responsibilities. By doing so, you can prioritize self-care, alleviate stress, and offer your mind and body the chance to rejuvenate.

Here are some suggestions of activities you can engage in over the weekend or on Sunday to rest your mind and body:

Write in a journal or planner.
Consider journaling or using a planner to declutter your mind. This will help you relax and reduce stress.

Meditate.
Engage in meditation to calm your body and mind while also focusing on your breathing.

Go for a hike or walk.
Take a leisurely walk or hike in nature. Exercise can be relaxing, especially when done in a way that's comfortable and enjoyable for you, such as walking by the beach or going on a hike with your dog.

Spend time with loved ones.
Spend quality time with loved ones. Socializing can still be a source of relaxation as long as it's something that you enjoy. Consider having a family game night, going out for drinks, or inviting friends over to watch the game.

Take a hot bath.
Take a hot bath to indulge in some self-care and enjoy some alone time. This can be enhanced with aromatherapy by using essential oils.

Read a book.
Read a book that you're interested in for personal reasons, not for work, school, or other responsibilities. This is a perfect way to relax in your favorite spot, whether that's a cozy couch or comfy bed.

You've Reached the End

Congratulations on completing this transformative journey toward a stress-free life. Your commitment to self-discovery and well-being is commendable. Remember that the knowledge within these pages is just the beginning. Embrace the practices you've learned, integrate them into your daily life, and allow them to foster a profound sense of peace and balance within. May this guide be the catalyst for a life filled with serenity and resilience.

Still Stressed?

If you find that despite implementing the tools and techniques outlined in this guide, you're still grappling with heightened stress levels, remember that you're not alone on this journey. Here are some additional resources you can explore:

1. **Local Support Groups: Check with community centers, local hospitals, or religious organizations for information on stress management support groups in your area.**
2. **Licensed Therapists or Counselors: Contact local mental health clinics, hospitals, or use online directories like Psychology Today (www.psychologytoday.com) to find licensed therapists or counselors specializing in stress management in your area.**
3. **Mental Health Hotlines:**
National Alliance on Mental Illness (NAMI) Helpline: 1-800-950-NAMI (6264)
Substance Abuse and Mental Health Services Administration (SAMHSA) Helpline: 1-800-662-HELP (4357)
Crisis Text Line: Text "HOME" to 741741 to connect with a crisis counselor.
4. **Online Mental Health Platforms:**
BetterHelp (www.betterhelp.com)
Talkspace (www.talkspace.com)
7 Cups (www.7cups.com)
5. **Stress Management Workshops: Contact local wellness centers, hospitals, or search for stress management workshops on platforms like Eventbrite (www.eventbrite.com) to find upcoming events in your area.**

A LETTER FROM *The Author*

In the whirlwind of modern life, stress has become an unwelcome companion, affecting our physical and mental well-being. Throughout this guide, we've delved into an array of natural methods to recognize, confront, and conquer this persistent force. By exploring the triggers, embracing mindful nutrition, incorporating the power of essential oils, and indulging in the rejuvenating practice of restorative yoga, we've unearthed an arsenal of tools to combat stress head-on.

Beyond these practices, we've delved into the intricate web of mental health, recognizing that stress is not just a temporary inconvenience but a complex interplay of factors that require ongoing attention and care. We've emphasized the significance of self-awareness and the cultivation of a resilient mindset, empowering you to navigate life's challenges with strength and grace.

As you set forth on your journey, remember that self-care is not a luxury; it's a fundamental necessity. Dedicate time to nurture your body, mind, and spirit, and honor the power of small, consistent steps. Let this guide serve as a blueprint for a more serene and balanced existence, where stress does not overshadow your inherent capacity for joy and well-being.

May you embark on a path illuminated by self-compassion, mindful living, and an unwavering commitment to your own holistic health. The journey towards a stress-free life begins with a single step, and today, you have taken a significant stride. Embrace this newfound knowledge, and may it pave the way for a life brimming with tranquility and vitality.

> "Life is a balance of holding on and letting go, and when it comes to stress, sometimes the most powerful action is inaction. In the stillness, you'll find your strength."
> — Unknown

With warmest wishes for your well-being,

NETIERA DANISE
#MENTAL

www.ingramcontent.com/pod-product-compliance
Lightning Source LLC
Chambersburg PA
CBHW080824280726
48660CB00019B/3809